Canadian Biography Series

WAYNE GRETZKY: THE GREAT ONE

Gretzky in action.

Wayne Gretzky

THE GREAT ONE

Gerald Redmond

ECW PRESS

Copyright © ECW PRESS, 1993

CANADIAN CATALOGUING IN PUBLICATION DATA

Redmond, Gerald, 1934–
Wayne Gretzky : the great one

(Canadian biography series)
Includes bibliographical references.
ISBN 1-55022-190-6

1. Gretzky, Wayne, 1961–   . 2. Hockey players –
Canada – Biography. I. Title. II. Series:
Canadian biography series (Toronto, Ont.).

GV848.5.G74R4 1993   796.962'092   C93-094543-3

This book has been published with the assistance of the
Ministry of Culture, Recreation and Tourism of the Province
of Ontario, through funds provided by the Ontario
Publishing Centre, and with the assistance of grants from
the Department of Communications, The Canada Council, the
Ontario Arts Council, and the Government of Canada through
the Canadian Studies and Special Projects Directorate of the
Department of the Secretary of State of Canada.

Design and imaging by ECW Type & Art, Oakville, Ontario.
Printed by Imprimerie Gagné, Louiseville, Québec.

Distributed by General Publishing Co. Limited,
30 Lesmill Road, Toronto, Ontario M3B 2T6,
(416) 445-3333, (800) 387-0172 (Canada), FAX (416) 445-5967.

Distributed to the trade in the United States exclusively by
InBook, 140 Commerce Street, P.O. Box 120261,
East Haven, Connecticut, U.S.A. 06512,
(203) 467-4257, FAX (203) 469-7697
Customer service: (800) 253-3605 or (800) 243-0138.

Published by ECW PRESS,
1980 Queen Street East, Toronto, Ontario M4L 1J2.

ACKNOWLEDGEMENTS

A number of people helped with this book. Thanks are due to Steve Knowles, Coordinator of Publications and Statistics of the Edmonton Oilers Hockey Club for access to archival material and photographs; to Paddy Lamb of the Edmonton City Archives for use of archival material and a photograph; to Gary Bartlett, Photo Editor of the *Edmonton Sun*, for access to the Gretzky file and use of photographs; to Lynne Colwell (Librarian) and Vicky White (Newsroom) of the *Expositor* (Brantford) for information and use of photographs; to Dr. Art Quinney, Dean of the Faculty of Physical Education and Recreation at the University of Alberta, for providing the Fitness Centre testing photograph, and to Dave Williams, Audio-Visual Supervisor of the same Faculty, for the photograph of the Gretzky statue; to Marlene Charters-Papple of the Wayne Gretzky Sports Centre in Brantford, for information; to Stacey Lorenz, doctoral student in Sport History at the University of Alberta, for his assistance in the location of some library materials; to Sam Abouhassan, Jim Matheson, Jock McKenzie, and Ken Powell, for Oilers tickets and information; to Carmen Bassett, my secretarial help in the Department of Physical Education and Sport Studies at the University of Alberta, for her efficient and sympathetic typing of the manuscript; to Käthe Roth of Montreal for her detailed copyediting of the same; to Robert Lecker and Holly Potter, of ECW PRESS, for their patience and understanding, particularly when the manuscript was delayed by the death of my father (to whom this book is dedicated); and as always to my wife Madge, The Great Companion.

PHOTOGRAPHS: Cover photo, frontispiece, illustrations 11, 12, and 15 are used by permission of the *Edmonton Sun*; illustrations 2 and 3 are used by permission of the *Expositor* (Brantford); illustration 4 is used by permission of Dr. H.A. Quinney; illustrations 5, 6, 7, 9, and 10 are used by permission of the Edmonton Oilers Hockey Club; illustrations 13 and 14 are used by permission of Dave Williams; illustration 16 is used by permission of the *Edmonton Journal*; and illustration 8 is used by permission of the City of Edmonton Archives.

ECW PRESS wishes to acknowledge the assistance of Frank Cosentino, a consultant to the Canadian Biography Series.

TABLE OF CONTENTS

LIST OF ILLUSTRATIONS

For
Edward John Redmond
("Ted")
1902–1992

Wayne Gretzky

THE GREAT ONE

BRANTFORD BOYHOOD

The town of Brantford, Ontario, named after Mohawk leader Joseph Brant, is located on the Grand River 104 kilometres southwest of Toronto. It was here that Alexander Graham Bell invented the telephone, and the first long-distance call was made from Brantford to Paris, Ontario, in 1876. Until recently, Brantford's historical link with this famous inventor was its main claim to fame, but now it is much better known for being the birthplace of Wayne Gretzky, as a sign on the road leading into town proudly proclaims.

Walter Gretzky worked for the Bell Telephone Company in Brantford. He and his wife, Phyllis, were living in an apartment when their first child, Wayne, was born, on 26 January 1961. Seven months later, the Gretzkys moved into a small house on Varadi Avenue, where the family grew with the addition of Kim (born in 1963), Keith (1966), Glen (1968), and Brent (1973).

But there were really two family homes. Wayne's grandparents, Tony and Mary Gretzky, owned a vegetable farm in Canning, Ontario. Tony had a White Russian background and Mary was Polish; Wayne's father was one of their six children, three boys and three girls, all of whom were born at home. With 25 acres and the Nith River running through it, the farm was an idyllic setting. Among other family amusements and pleasures, it offered skating in the winter, and swimming and fishing in the summer. Walter Gretzky remembers it as "a special place,

11

first to grow up in, then to bring up our own kids," and recalls, "We practically lived on the farm. We'd drive out after supper and spend just about every weekend there."

One of the winter weekend rituals for the Gretzky family was watching *Hockey Night in Canada* on television on Saturday nights. It was then that young Wayne gave the first hint of latent talent and future ambition, running around the living room using a souvenir hockey stick to shoot a rubber ball past designated (and seated) goalie Grandma's legs. Two months before his third birthday, Wayne had his first skate on the Nith River, and he was soon skating on the outdoor rink in a park near his home as well. Wayne confesses to a "serious addiction" around this time, always staying on the ice for as long as he possibly could until his cold, and patient, father took him home. Walter soon made a rink in the backyard of the Gretzky home. Four-year-old Wayne and his friends made sure that the "Wally Coliseum" was well used, especially after Walter strung lights from a clothesline, and it soon became a sort of neighbourhood playground. Walter could now watch from the warmth of the kitchen, when he wasn't outside giving his son advice. Phyllis was generally supportive of her son's addiction, but Walter recalls that she put her foot down once when she refused to go out again shopping for a lawn sprinkler in the middle of winter!

Phyllis had met Walter when he was playing Junior B hockey, and sport was a natural part of Gretzky family life; both believed that it provided the social benefits of participation as well as physical exercise. Wayne's unbridled enthusiasm was matched by his parents' unfailing encouragement. In particular, Walter Gretzky revealed himself to be an astute teacher, developing interesting drills and practices to feed his son's insatiable appetite for hockey. Empty detergent bottles served as pylons for Wayne to skate around, targets were set up in the net for forehand and backhand shots, and sometimes a harder-to-control tennis ball was used instead of a puck.

Walter never had to push Wayne to excel; in fact, he often had to pull his son off the ice to eat and sleep. As Wayne says in his autobiography, "All I wanted to do in the winters was be on the ice. I'd get up in the morning, skate from 7:00 to 8:30, go to school, come home at 3:30, stay on the ice until my mom insisted I come in for dinner, eat in my skates, then go back out until 9:00."

Even given Wayne's dedication and supreme natural ability, Walter's innovative coaching of sound techniques, and a loving and stable home environment, no one could have predicted Wayne's ultimate and incredible achievements in hockey. But before he had scored his first goal on a real team, all of these factors had combined in his young life to form what could be called the Great Beginning.

First Goals

By the time he was six, Wayne writes, "I was driving my parents bananas" to find him a real hockey team to play with. But boys had to be 10 years old to play minor hockey in Brantford, and so Wayne had to be satisfied with a few hours a day on the backyard rink, sharpening his basic skills. Then, a few weeks before the 1967–68 season, a newspaper notice announced tryouts for the Novice A Division Nadrofsky Steelers, of the Brantford Atom League. Six-year-old Wayne looked lost among the taller 10-year-olds — until he was on the ice. Coach Dick Martin ignored his age and size and selected him for the team. In his first season, he wore number 11, played on the third line, and scored just one goal. Assistant coach Bob Phillips assured him that there would be "lots more after this," not realizing just how prophetic those words would be. When Wayne cried after the year-end banquet, disconsolate because everyone had won a trophy but him, his father made a prediction that he never forgot: "Wayne, keep practicing and one day you're gonna have so many trophies, we're not gonna have room for them all."

It was around this time that a Gretzky trademark was born. Because the team sweater was much too large for young Wayne, it was always getting caught on his stick on his shooting side. One day his father tucked the left side into his pants, and it has been there ever since.

The following season with the Steelers, Wayne scored 27 goals; the next year, when he turned eight, he scored 104; during the 1970–71 season, he scored 196. He played everywhere but in goal, mostly on defence, but often in a forward position when a goal was needed. In one particular game, with the Steelers trailing 3–0, Wayne was called upon to get his team back in the game; he responded by scoring three consecutive goals (a "hat trick") in just 45 seconds. As one of his biographers, Stephen Hanks, has written, "Young Wayne Gretzky was developing a pattern that would continue into his professional career — that of always seeming able to top himself." During the 1971–72 season, 10-year-old Wayne, four feet four inches tall and weighing 70 pounds, scored an incredible 378 goals, still easily a record for that age group. Bear in mind, too, that these are goals, not total points. When assists are added to Wayne's statistics (63 in 1969–70, 120 in 1970–71), the figures are even more remarkable.

Outside of his hockey exploits, Wayne was an "ordinary kid," living a life like that of many other Canadian youngsters, according to Gretzky biographer Fred McFadden. Summers, he fished and swam in the river at his grandparents' farm. A good student at Greenbrier School, in Brantford, he entertained thoughts of becoming an architect or an engineer. But he was also a star athlete in such sports as baseball and lacrosse. Walter Gretzky writes, proudly,

In the summer of 1971, coming off the 196-goal hockey season, Wayne scored 158 goals and added 66 assists in 31 games for Brantford PUC in the inter-city lacrosse league, pitched and played baseball in the house league and for Brantford Shanghai in the inter-county tyke baseball league. Was anyone else playing three sports as well?

The answer, of course, was no. But young Wayne's athletic versatility was resented by some, and he reports in his autobiography that "Gretzky-bashing" became relentless "in every sport I played as a kid."

The Price of Fame

By 1970, Wayne was playing for both minor novice and major novice teams, and playing tournament hockey in both divisions as well, moving happily from team to team. In the 1970–71 season, the highest-scoring line in hockey was a trio of nine-year-olds — Wayne Gretzky, Chris Halyk, and Ron Jamula — who notched a total of 313 points. Wayne's feats were attracting attention far beyond Brantford, and he quickly became a national celebrity. As S.H. Burchard put it in *Sports Star: Wayne Gretzky*, "He got used to being famous at a young age." But along with the adulation and publicity, Wayne was finding that there was a price to pay for his fame.

By the time he was 10, Wayne had done more interviews than some National Hockey League players, and been labelled "the Great Gretzky" in a London, Ontario, newspaper. (This nickname was supposedly borrowed from the F. Scott Fitzgerald novel *The Great Gatsby*.) Posters advertising out-of-town tournaments were using his name as an attraction. When he was 11, Wayne was featured in a two-page spread in the April 1972 issue of *Canadian Magazine*, and he sat at the head table at the 1972 Kiwanis "Great Men of Sport" dinner in Brantford. Among the many celebrities present was NHL star Gordie Howe, who was young Wayne's hero (and even more so when he rescued Wayne from having to make an unanticipated speech). The meeting began a friendship between these two hockey greats of different eras, which continues to this day.

Predictably, such stardom didn't sit too well with a number of people, especially some other hockey parents. The talented youngster was sometimes booed and called a "puck hog" or "hotdogger," and coaches and referees were accused of favouritism where he was concerned. When he was just nine years old, he once had to have a police escort to a play-off game in Welland because some teenagers had threatened to beat him up. As the pressure became worse, Wayne was reduced to tears on more than one occasion. He recalls in his autobiography, "I had seen adults at their best and their worst. I learned that jealousy is the worst disease in life. . . . And I decided one more thing. I wanted to get out of that town."

Meanwhile, Wayne's hockey career continued to blossom. As an underaged newcomer in major peewee hockey with Turkstra Lumber, he scored 105 goals in the 1972–73 season and 192 goals the following season, including goal number 1,000, which he scored during his team's 8–1 win over Waterford on 10 April 1974. He was 13 years old.

In 1974–75, playing with the major bantam team the Charcon Chargers (though he was still at the age to be playing minor bantam), in his final season of minor hockey, he scored 90 goals. But the Gretzky-bashing was getting worse. Walter Gretzky suggests that the "capper" came on 2 February 1975, "Brantford Day" at Maple Leaf Gardens in Toronto, when 14-year-old Wayne was booed as he skated out onto the ice. In any event, it signalled the end of Wayne's boyhood in Brantford. Soon afterwards, he left home to play hockey.

TEENAGE PRODIGY

By the time Wayne was 14, the Metropolitan Toronto Hockey League was showing an interest in his considerable talents; when family friend Sam McMaster, who was in charge of the Young Nationals (an organization that operated teams in all divisions of the MTHL), suggested that Wayne move to Toronto to play, the youngster was excited at the prospect. His parents, however, were worried about the effect of life in the big city on a teenage boy, and Wayne had to convince them that he was responsible enough not to be led astray. Arrangements were made for Wayne to stay with friends, Bill and Rita Cormish, as their legal ward, to comply with residency regulations in minor hockey. Wayne was enrolled as a student in West Humber Collegiate Institute, in Etobicoke, in the summer of 1975, and was looking forward to his first hockey season outside of Brantford.

However, the move turned out to be more complicated than anticipated. The Ontario Minor Hockey Association was not satisfied with Wayne's new residency status, and the Gretzkys had to appeal to the parent body, the Ontario Hockey Asso-

FIGURE 2

*Eleven-year-old Wayne with the
Brantford Nadrofsky Steelers, 1972.*

ciation, as well as to the Canadian Amateur Hockey Association. The solution turned out to be Junior B hockey, presenting Wayne's parents with yet another worry: the fact that Wayne would be playing against 20-year-olds. They were persuaded that their son would survive, even though Walter thought that Wayne looked like "a calf in a herd of buffalo" in his first Junior B game. (Still, the calf scored two goals and was even used on a penalty-killing unit when his team, the Vaughan Nationals, was two men short.) "So," his father recalls, "after a court case, six months of bickering and enough turmoil to give us all ulcers, the simple little move to Toronto was accomplished."

That year, Wayne scored 27 goals and 33 assists and won the Metro Junior B Hockey League Rookie-of-the-Year award. He also excelled for his school team in midget basketball, helping it to win the championship as the leading points scorer. The following year, playing hockey with the Seneca Nationals, Wayne did better, scoring 36 goals and 26 assists in just 32 games.

Although he was happy with his accomplishments, he often felt homesick, so he called his family frequently and went home most weekends. Looking back on this period, Wayne regrets that he wasn't around to see his brother Brent grow up: "To him, for quite a while, I'm afraid I wasn't so much a big brother as a hockey superstar who spent the night now and again." The Cormishes were true friends and model foster parents during his two years in Toronto, and refused payment not only for his lodging but also for providing a second home for Kim, who stayed with them for two years while she attended school. (Years later, when Wayne was a superstar, he insisted on sending the Cormishes to Hawaii for a holiday, the only payment they ever accepted.)

Barring injury, there was never any doubt that Wayne would become a professional hockey player, and soon another family friend, Gus Badali, was acting as his agent. Many clubs were keeping an eye on the young Gretzky, their interest increasing when he turned 16 and became eligible for Junior A hockey — and even more so when, at the end of the 1976–77 season, he was rated second only to Steve Peters of the Peterborough Petes, on a list of players ranked according to their potential. Now the

FIGURE 3

Wayne with his idol Gordie Howe, at the Kiwanis
"Great Men of Sports" dinner, Brantford, 1972.

question was, which team would draft the 16-year-old wonder? Wayne's parents wanted him closer to home, if possible, so Walter Gretzky wrote letters to discourage faraway teams from drafting his son. Wayne himself would have preferred to play for the nearby Peterborough Petes. But Angelo Bumbacco, general manager of the Soo Greyhounds of Sault Ste. Marie, persevered against the Gretzkys' reluctance, drafted Wayne with his third pick, and persuaded the family to visit the town, 800 kilometres from Brantford. An assurance of plenty of playing time, a provision in the contract for a university education should Wayne not make the team or be injured, and a fortuitous arrangement for him to live with former Brantford residents Jim and Sylvia Bodnar (Wayne had played with their son, Steve, in peewee and novice), were the main factors in their decision. Young Wayne would play in "the Soo," hometown of NHL superstar Phil Esposito, who had scored a record 76 goals with the Boston Bruins in the 1970–71 season.

Number 99 and Nicknames

When he arrived in Sault Ste. Marie, Wayne was a cocky yet naïve teenager. At his first Greyhounds practice, he asked the coach, Muzz MacPherson, how many points the Junior A scoring champion had got the year before. When Muzz told him 170, Wayne said, "No problem. I'll break that." (He did, scoring 182 points, but still came second in the scoring race behind 19-year-old Bobby Smith, of Ottawa, with 192 points.) His life was divided primarily between high school ("great in math, terrible in English," he claims) and hockey, with a daily trip to a favourite hangout near the rink for apple pie and ice cream.

Another Gretzky trademark originated during his time with the Soo Greyhounds: his use of sweater number 99. Wayne had coveted number 9, the one worn by his idol, Gordie Howe (and by other NHL stars Maurice Richard and Bobby Hull), but it was already taken. He tried numbers 14 and 19, but he didn't feel comfortable with them. Then MacPherson suggested that he try number 99, pointing out that Phil Esposito and Ken Hodge, who had recently been traded to the New York Rangers, had adopted numbers 77 and 88, respectively. Wayne was dubious at first, fearing ridicule and opponents running at him, but MacPherson told him, "They're going to be running at you anyway." So Wayne allowed himself to be convinced, survived the initial razzing and skepticism, and has worn number 99 ever since.

Long before the terms "Number 99" or "the Great One" became common currency, Wayne's exploits were attracting nicknames. His teammates in the Soo (all of them older than he was) started calling him "Ink" because of all the publicity that he was getting — profiles in magazines such as *Sports Illustrated*, *Maclean's*, and *Weekend*, articles in local and national newspapers (and even the *New York Times*), and radio and television interviews. Another nickname was "Pretzel." Wayne says that this was because he skates "kind of hunched over," while his father maintains that it was because they thought they could break him about that easily. But the generally accepted moniker was "the Great Gretzky," and the term soon became popular with the electronic and print media.

Wayne was now being paid $75 a week, but the Greyhounds were getting a handsome return on their investment, with attendance at home games doubling to about 2,500 spectators per game. Wayne was a good draw on the road, too, with cities such as Hamilton, Ottawa, and Peterborough boasting their largest crowds of the season when he was in town. He set a Junior A record for most goals and points in a season by a rookie (and won the Rookie-of-the-Year award), and led the league with seven shorthanded goals, 21 multiple-goal games, and no fewer than seven hat tricks. He was unanimously voted the league's "smartest player," received the coaches' nod as "most dangerous in the play area" and "best playmaker," and led all players with 20 assists in 13 games in the play-offs. Beyond his extraordinary skill, Wayne's sportsmanship was also recognized when he was awarded the Bill Hanley Trophy as the league's "most gentlemanly player."

Future Prospects

Even with these numbers to his credit, some scouts still considered 17-year-old Wayne too scrawny, at 161 pounds, to play in the National Hockey League. They also thought that his shot and his skating could be better, and wondered about his defensive capabilities. Others, however, believed that he was a great prospect and a unique talent, with his uncanny anticipation and peripheral vision and his stickhandling, playmaking, and passing abilities. If his shot lacked some power, it was certainly an accurate one — and for a "slow" skater, he somehow consistently got past opponents. As the debate over his future continued, even Wayne tended to sell himself short, saying, "Mentally, I'm ready for the pros, but physically I'm not."

But if his dream of playing in the NHL seemed to be on hold, or perhaps even doubtful, at least there was an alternative opportunity. For "the pros" now included an "upstart" league, the World Hockey Association (formed in 1971), which was challenging the established league. To do this, it was signing younger players (since 1963 the NHL had had an agreement with the Canadian Amateur Hockey Association that it would not sign juniors under 20 years of age) and enticing some well-known NHL stars to its ranks through lucrative contracts. The signing of Bobby Hull to the Winnipeg Jets provided credibility, and the Houston Aeros acquired Gordie Howe to play alongside his sons Mark and Marty. Canada was well-represented in the new league, with teams in Edmonton, Ottawa, Quebec City, and Winnipeg. The WHA was therefore very much a factor in the discussions over Wayne's future. To some of the league's entrepreneurs, he represented the perfect underage junior prospect, and even the continuing speculation over his possible physical shortcomings would provide welcome publicity.

On 12 February 1978, another decisive factor entered the equation, when Muzz MacPherson resigned as coach of the Soo Greyhounds over some personal problems with management, and Paul Theriault was hired. Wayne had enjoyed the MacPherson way of doing things and wasn't enamoured of Theriault's more rigid and constricting coaching style, even going so far as to say, in his autobiography, "I hated the guy. Without Muzz,

The Soo suddenly felt a lot colder." Three more years of junior hockey in order to qualify for the NHL (and possible drafting by the last-place team) now seemed a much less attractive prospect than taking his chances with the WHA.

Young Professional in a New League

Wayne was the youngest player in the national team competing in the junior-hockey world championship, played in Montreal in December of 1977, and had impressed the professional scouts by leading all scorers with eight goals and nine assists in six games and being the only Canadian player named to the tournament all-star team. The first offers from WHA teams came from the Birmingham Bulls (whose owner, John F. Bassett, had a longtime association with Wayne's agent, Gus Badali) and the New England Whalers (the team for which Gordie Howe was now playing), but it was the Indianapolis Racers that obtained his services in the end, with Vancouver-based owner Nelson Skalbania "making the Gretzky family an offer they couldn't refuse," according to Gretzky biographers Joseph Romain and James Duplacey. Wayne, Badali, and his parents were flown to Vancouver by private jet and given the royal treatment — and Wayne impressed Skalbania-the-jogger with his fitness over a trial run of several miles — before he signed a four-year package worth almost a million dollars. With this ambition realized, there was much to celebrate in the Gretzky family, especially considering that Wayne had worked the previous summer pouring gravel in potholes for $5 an hour.

Wayne's professional début, however, was certainly no cause for celebration, and it revived some familiar criticisms regarding his chances in the professional ranks. One of Skalbania's contacts in Houston expressed doubts about Wayne's skating ability before he ever played for the Racers, and his performance in Indianapolis was ordinary by his standards. He played in only eight games, scoring just three goals and three assists, hardly a promising return on Skalbania's investment or calculated to bring the city's dwindling hockey audience back to the stadium.

A promotional blitz and a "Great Gretzky Fan Club" failed to generate bigger crowds, and Skalbania, on the brink of financial disaster, soon realized that he couldn't afford to keep Wayne. He tried selling the young player to the Winnipeg Jets, but was refused; he then quickly entered desperate negotiations with former partner Peter Pocklington, owner of the WHA Edmonton Oilers. Ironically, Wayne's first two goals as a professional hockey player had come in the fifth game of the season, against those very Oilers!

Although he was settling in comfortably at Indianapolis, boarding with Dr. Terry Frederick and his family, attending night classes at Broad Ripple High School, and enjoying his new sports car, Wayne anticipated that a move might be necessary and was not surprised when it happened. Only 53 days after training camp had opened for the Indianapolis Racers, Wayne became an Edmonton Oiler, when Pocklington paid $850,000 for him, winger Peter Driscoll, and goalkeeper Eddie Mio. Mio later joked, in the *Edmonton Sun*, that "$849,999.99 was for Gretz and one cent for me and Peter."

An Impressive Début

Wayne accepted an offer from Oilers coach Glen Sather to live with him until he got settled, and he soon impressed his host with both his hockey skills and his healthy appetite — Sather maintained that Wayne ate more than his whole family and was always ready for snacks. Then the young player moved in with Ray Bodnar and his wife; Ray was the brother of Jim Bodnar, with whom Wayne had lived in the Soo. "His favorite thing at our house was the microwave," Bodnar recalled in Stephen Hanks's Gretzky biography. Even so, Wayne's new Thunderbird was often seen parked outside some of Edmonton's well-known eateries. Small wonder that by now Wayne had grown to six feet, weighed 170 pounds, and was putting on muscle.

It was around this time that Wayne and teammate Kevin Lowe walked into a lounge where an aspiring young singer named Vikki Moss was on stage. Afterwards, Wayne asked her if she would like a drink but, as Vikki was only 17 years old, they settled for coffee. Vikki had nine brothers, Wayne had three, and they found that they had other things in common. Thus began a relationship that lasted for the next seven years.

The Edmonton media had adopted the "Great Gretzky" tag and Wayne didn't disappoint them, the Oilers's fans, or team management. In his first 12 games for the Oilers, he scored six goals and eight assists. The Oilers had a record of one win and four losses when he arrived, but the team then went on an 11–4 winning streak in their next 15 games. Wayne was getting standing ovations for his passing and stickhandling skills, and even for his skating, and was receiving ringing endorsements all round. Anxious to secure his protégé, Pocklington signed Wayne to an unprecedented 21-year deal. Wayne was to receive $3 million over the first 10 years, with options until 1999 — "the longest contract in the history of professional sports," as Gretzky biographer S.H. Burchard termed it. The contract was signed at a ceremony at centre ice in Northlands Coliseum on 26 January 1979, Wayne's eighteenth birthday.

Edmonton had led WHA attendance the previous season and now, with Gretzky on board, seemed a sure bet to be one of the teams selected to join the NHL if the two leagues were to merge. A delighted Pocklington showed every confidence in his expensive acquisition, predicting superstar status for Wayne in the years ahead; Glen Sather echoed these sentiments, telling Wayne that he would be captain of an NHL Oilers team one day. A mutual respect had developed between the coach and his star player, which survived occasional differences. Sather admired Wayne's comeback attitude, and Wayne liked his coach's coolness and competitive nature.

Wayne did his best to justify his huge salary by helping the Oilers achieve success in the WHA. He finished his first pro season in third place in league scoring, with 46 goals and 110 points, and won the Rookie-of-the-Year award. A personal highlight during the season was being selected to centre Gordie Howe and his son Mark in a three-game series between the WHA All-Stars and the Moscow Dynamo, the élite Soviet team. The Oilers finished the regular season in first place and reached the final round of the play-offs, but lost the Avco Cup to the Winnipeg Jets, four games to two. Wayne led all players in play-off scoring with 10 goals and 20 points.

A Marriage of Convenience

In March of 1979, after intense and prolonged negotiations, the expensive seven-year war between the NHL and the WHA came to an end. In the ensuing marriage of convenience — "expansion" was the preferred term to "merger" for diplomatic and legal reasons — four of the existing WHA teams, the Edmonton Oilers, the Hartford (previously New England) Whalers, the Quebec Nordiques, and the Winnipeg Jets, would become part of the NHL. The WHA would cease operations following its 1979 play-offs, and the NHL's four new clubs would begin play in the 1979–80 season. To allow underage juniors who had signed WHA contracts to play in the new 21-team league, the NHL lowered its draft age to 18. Thus, in the complicated expansion draft of 1979, the Edmonton Oilers had to reclaim Gretzky as an underage junior, and then protect him as a priority choice — not that this was any chore, under the circumstances. Stephen Hanks quotes Oilers general manager Larry Gordon, who echoed the sentiments of many Edmonton hockey fans when he said, "We've got the guy to build a team around. Now we've just got to give him some help." Those same fans eagerly bought up more than 15,000 season tickets in 11 days.

In the National
Hockey League

Attributing Wayne Gretzky's success in hockey up to 1979 to luck seems incredibly myopic in retrospect. Nevertheless, the word "fluke" was conjured up in several quarters to describe his progress toward his NHL début. In his autobiography, Wayne describes how one user of the term conceded his ability to play

26

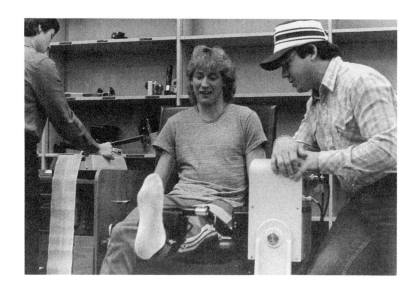

FIGURE 4

*Eighteen-year-old Wayne undergoes leg strength
tests at the University of Alberta Fitness Laboratory.*

junior varsity hockey, but questioned what would happen to him in the NHL. Stephen Hanks, in his Gretzky biography, writes that the NHL did little to advertise its new star: "Instead, the NHL's muckamucks echoed the same skepticism of Gretzky that he'd heard since his days in Junior hockey. The kid's too small. The kid's too scrawny. The kid won't withstand the tough checking in the NHL. The kid will be lucky to score 20 goals." And in the *1991 NHL 75th Anniversary Commemorative Book*, Jay Teitel writes, "From the vantage point of the generation I belonged to, there was no way Wayne Gretzky could be anything but a fluke. He could not be for real. Hence the doubt." Wayne was determined to answer his persistent critics once and for all by proving himself in the NHL. This league, established in 1917 with only four teams, had grown to represent the most-respected athletic rite of passage for Canadian boys in what is Canada's true national sport.

The First NHL Season

Wayne's first season in the NHL was remarkable in many ways, as fulfilled expectations in some quarters were mixed with disappointments in others. It was never less than interesting, and in the end he repaid the Oilers's confidence in full and raised hopes for the future. It was his fifth straight year as a rookie (from 1975 to 1978, he had played in the Junior B, Junior A, OHA, and WHA leagues), and he was following in the footsteps of Gordie Howe and Bobby Orr, who had also entered the NHL ranks as 18-year-olds.

Wayne's performance was all the more creditable considering that he was plagued with tonsillitis for most of the season, and was living on throat lozenges, aspirin, and penicillin. (His tonsils were removed in a Paris, Ontario, hospital, where he was admitted under the name of "Smith," after the season ended.) After a relatively slow start (his first goal didn't come until the Oilers's fifth game, against Vancouver) by midseason, Wayne led the Oilers's scoring by a large margin, and was ranked fifth in the NHL scoring race. Although the Oilers were in last place, their fans could find many signs of encouragement in the exploits of their franchise player. A summary of Wayne's first NHL season, in a Gretzky biography by Jane Mersky Leder, reads:

> He scored two goals and an assist in early November to help the Oilers defeat the powerful New York Islanders, 7–5. One night in February 1980, he tied a thirty-three-year-old record by getting seven assists in a single game. In that same game against the Washington Capitals, he set a single-season record for a rookie by getting his 96th point. A few days later, he became the youngest player ever to get 100 points in a season. . . . On April 2, he became the youngest player to score 50 goals in a season!

This is not to mention another impressive Oilers victory, 7–5, over the Toronto Maple Leafs, in which Wayne had two goals and four assists, and passes over the fact that Wayne was selected for the all-star game. There were many other highlights in that season. With pirouettes, passes from behind the opponents' nets, and accurate backhands and slap shots, the Gretzky repertoire of moves was exciting hockey fans and converting doubters into believers.

However, some saw deficiencies in Wayne's defensive capabilities. When it looked as if the Oilers might not make the play-offs, veteran defenceman Pat Price told Wayne that he had to play better defence. Wayne replied that he was doing his best to help the team, saying, "I can't do it any other way." Fortunately, Sather was an astute enough coach to allow the prodigy to do things his way, employing what teammate Kevin Lowe called "the Stallion Theory": don't rein him in, let him run and do what he does best.

What Wayne did best, of course, was accumulate a large number of goals and assists, helping the Oilers to win nine of their last 10 games to finish with 69 points and clinch a play-off berth. Wayne finished his first NHL season with 51 goals and 86 assists, for an impressive total of 137 points. This tied him for the league lead in scoring with Marcel Dionne, of the Los Angeles Kings, but the Art Ross Trophy was awarded to Dionne because he had scored 53 goals during the season, two more than Wayne.

The First Awards

Although Wayne did not win the Art Ross Trophy in 1980, the winner was gracious about his achievement: Marcel Dionne said that he would polish the trophy up because he knew that Wayne Gretzky would be winning it several times in the future. Wayne appreciated the compliment, but the fact that the award had not been shared rankled, because he felt that his higher assists total demonstrated an unselfishness that is absolutely essential in the team sport of hockey. Wayne's father also acknowledged Dionne's professionalism and sportsmanship, but he was more upset, pointing out that the NHL had also changed the eligibility rules for the Calder Trophy, awarded "to the player selected as the most proficient in his first year of competition in the National Hockey League," such that WHA statistics didn't count in NHL totals, but ex-WHA players weren't eligible for Rookie-of-the-Year honours in the NHL because they had played in a professional league. This meant that Wayne's season in the WHA would count as a year in pro hockey, making him ineligible to be NHL rookie of the year — even though his WHA points would not count toward his career totals! In his book, Walter Gretzky discusses this contradiction at some length as one indication of the lingering antagonism the NHL harboured toward the defunct WHA.

While these decisions pertaining to the Art Ross and Calder trophies may not have been directed against Wayne personally, father and son soon became aware that but for these changes, Wayne might have swept every major award available to him in the NHL, in his very first season. For, amazingly, Wayne did win the Hart Memorial Trophy, awarded "to the player adjudged to be the most valuable to his team," a most prestigious recognition, since it is decided by a poll of the Professional Hockey Writers Association in all of the NHL cities at the end of the regular schedule. Wayne was the only "rookie" ever to win it, and it remains one of his proudest achievements. He also won the Lady Byng Trophy, awarded "to the player adjudged to have exhibited the best type of sportsmanship and gentlemanly conduct combined with a high standard of playing ability," and was proud to join other great players who had won this award, including Bobby Hull, Stan Mikita, and Gilbert Perrault.

Wayne's statistics and awards at the end of the 1979–80 season gave ample proof that his was the most successful début ever in the NHL. As Walter Gretzky wrote, "The NHL and the fans knew now that the Oilers were for real, and Wayne had answered the people who doubted that he would star in the NHL. Like it or not, the NHL *Guide* was about to get an overhaul. It was only a matter of time." Yet no one, not even the most ardent of Gretzky converts and fans, could possibly have envisaged just how much of an "overhaul" Wayne would ultimately be responsible for. Who would have dared to forecast, for instance, that his 1980 Hart Trophy would be but the first of no fewer than nine such awards, including eight years in a row, from 1980 to 1987, or that the Art Ross Trophy, which had eluded him at the end of his first season, would be indisputably his for seven consecutive seasons, from 1981 to 1987?

The fact is, at the beginning of the 1980s, the NHL had a genius on the ice who was starting to redefine the limits of a player's ability, and to rewrite the record book and hockey history. If the NHL *Guide* was regarded as the "Hockey Bible," then in future, like its namesake, it could be divided into two distinct periods: "Before Gretzky" and "After Gretzky." By the end of the decade, it would be obvious that no other athlete anywhere had ever dominated the record books of a team sport in such a manner and to such an extent.

Social Life in Edmonton

Wayne was also enjoying life in Edmonton off the ice. He had always lived with families during his hockey career, but by this time he wanted a place of his own. Sather decided it would be a good idea for him to live with the Oilers first-ever draft choice, Kevin Lowe. As Lowe said, "Wayne and I got along famously from Day One in our south side apartment." Their compatibility was enhanced by their common dedication to becoming the best hockey players they could be in the shortest possible time, and by Wayne's admission of his roommate's superior cooking ability. Lowe appreciated Wayne's down-to-earth, unaffected manner, while Wayne had great respect for Lowe.

Lowe admits, "In the early days Gretz and I were dazzled by big-league life"; indeed, they were often seen dining at Edmonton's finest restaurants. Wayne would often be interrupted by autograph seekers, and he would oblige, but would always hand the paper over for Kevin to sign as well. (In later years, when the demands simply became too great, he would insist on being allowed to finish his meal before complying with the request.) Watching television, both at home and on the road, also became a regular form of relaxation for both hockey players. Wayne impressed Kevin with his expert analysis of baseball games, and also with his detailed recall of the plots of various soap operas.

Dave Lumley and Doug Hicks moved into the same building as Wayne and Lowe; Mark Messier, who lived in the suburbs, became a regular visitor. Hicks was a seasoned professional by the time he reached Edmonton, via Minnesota and Chicago, and, in Lowe's words, he "knew the meaning of teamsmanship." Among the ways in which he broadened the younger players's horizons was to introduce them to the "instant vacation." Immediately after the Oilers were eliminated from the 1980 play-offs by the Philadelphia Flyers, Hicks persuaded Wayne, Kevin, Mark, and Dave to fly to Hawaii for a holiday. They were a bit taken aback at first by the spontaneity of it all, but the vacation was a timely respite from the rigours of that first NHL season and the regimentation of travelling from city to city for seven months of the year, and a welcome escape from team curfews.

Young Wayne was cultivating some important, enduring friendships — especially with Kevin Lowe and Mark Messier — learning to enjoy the benefits of his fame and fortune, and adjusting to his new responsibilities. Although the publicity and status would likely turn the head of any 19-year-old, he impressed those around him with his courteous and sensible behaviour. Wayne Gretzky, the superstar on the ice, was moulding a similar image outside the rink. But hockey was still the main passion and purpose in his life, and the focus of some unfulfilled ambitions. Wayne looked forward eagerly to his second season in the NHL.

The Second Season: 1980–81

Harry Sinden, general manager of the Boston Bruins and coach of Team Canada in the 1972 series against the USSR, observed that if opponents thought Wayne Gretzky was trouble now, "just wait until he's a part of a good team." Well, the Oilers enjoyed possibly the best draft in NHL history before the next season began. They obtained 19-year-old defenceman Paul Coffey with their first-round pick; 20-year-old right-winger Jari Kurri, a Finn, in the second round; speedy 20-year-old left-winger Glenn Anderson in the third; and talented goaltender Andy Moog in the seventh. Along with Lowe and Messier, these players formed the nucleus of a team that was now ready to challenge any other team in the league. As much as anything, this was a tribute to the astute homework of Oilers scout Barry Fraser.

The young Oilers started the season well, even though Wayne himself was suffering somewhat from having to adapt to some relentless shadowing by opponents, the price of his accomplishments in the previous season. Large, rugged Dave Semenko, the team's "enforcer," played on Wayne's line, acting as his "bodyguard," and in one stretch even scored six goals in seven games. There was some frustration and worry at midseason, when the team was floundering at fifth place in the six-team Smythe Division. Still, Wayne was again tied with Dionne for the lead in the scoring race (and again Dionne was given the halfway-point $500 prize money on the basis of more goals). Then, in late February, 1981, the Oilers defeated the Philadelphia Flyers, a.k.a. "the Broad Street Bullies," for the first time. The Oilers had fallen behind 2–0 in the second period, but in the last 21

33

minutes of the game, Wayne scored two goals and added two assists, to lead his team to a 6-2 victory. Down the stretch, Number 99 was obviously ready to begin another assault on the NHL record book.

Wayne broke Phil Esposito's single-season points total record of 152 (on 30 March) and Bobby Orr's single-season assist record of 102 (on 1 April) in the same week. He scored 34 goals in the last 40 games, and notched five goals and two assists in one game against the St. Louis Blues. His five points in the season finale, on 4 April, gave him 55 goals and a record 109 assists, for a record 164 points. This made Wayne the youngest player, at the age of 20 years, to win the Art Ross Trophy as the NHL's scoring champion. That 164th point also gave him 301 for his first two seasons, making him the quickest 300-point scorer in league history. Led by Wayne, the Oilers won 11 out of their last 12 games to finish in fourth place in the Smythe Division, just four points out of second spot, and fourteenth in the league.

The Oilers were to face the fabled Canadiens, in a series starting at the Montreal Forum, in the five-game first round of the play-offs. It was an awe-inspiring prospect for a young expansion team from the West, and the Montreal goalie, Richard Sévigny, predicted that the Canadiens's popular right-wing superstar Guy Lafleur would put Wayne Gretzky in his pocket. Sather cannily underplayed the Oilers's chances, so that his young team was loose, ready, and not feeling too much pressure. To everyone's surprise, the Oilers swept the Canadiens in three straight games, winning 6–3 and 3–1 at the Forum, and 6–2 back at Northlands Coliseum. Wayne contributed in spectacular fashion to these unanticipated heroics, scoring five assists (a play-off record) in the first game and three goals and an assist in the third.

The Oilers's reward for their victory was a second-round seven-game series against the defending Stanley Cup champions, the New York Islanders, in which they were beaten — but not embarrassed — by a final tally of four games to two. Wayne scored a hat trick during the Oilers's 5–2 win in game three at the Northlands Coliseum, which gained him some media attention, but he had made headlines of a different sort before the series had even begun.

During a press conference before the opening game at Long Island, when asked about the Oilers's upset over the Canadiens, Wayne replied, "We had to be prepared mentally and physically to beat the best team in hockey." It was an honest enough opinion, and certainly true enough in terms of hockey history. In a 24-year span, between 1955 and 1979, the Canadiens had compiled an amazing record of 15 Stanley Cup victories, including the only run ever of five in a row. But Wayne could not have anticipated how those five words — "the best team in hockey" — would be seized upon by the New York reporters and used as ammunition to motivate the Islanders against their upstart opponents. An anti-Gretzky bandwagon gained momentum, and *New York Times* Pulitzer Prize-winning columnist Dave Anderson wrote, "For all his precocious genius on the ice Wayne Gretzky is indisputably 20 years old in coping with the psychology of play-off diplomacy. By complimenting the Canadiens, he unthinkingly has insulted the Islanders."

Nothing, however, could mar Wayne's tremendous season. He won his second Hart Trophy, was named the league's first-team all-star centre, and became the first NHL player to average more than two points per game. The accolades poured in, and Wayne himself was more than satisfied about the way things had gone. In his autobiography, he writes, "It was an unforgettable season. It was the thrill of my life. Everything I'd ever wanted was coming true. I was playing big-time NHL hockey with a team that was improving all the time, and I was proving I could stay with anybody."

Wayne's euphoria at the conclusion of the NHL season was short-lived, however. During the 1981 Canada Cup Tournament, accolades were few and far between, and criticisms were many and varied.

Nothing about the 1981 Canada Cup experience appealed to Wayne. He devotes considerable space in his autobiography to criticizing the "boot camp" atmosphere, the poor organization with too many coaches, and his own inept play (despite centring a line with Guy Lafleur and Gilbert Perrault). He also suffered some injuries in a particularly rough game against Sweden. Although he finished the tournament as individual scoring leader with a total of 12 points (five goals and seven assists), the

Soviets trounced Team Canada 8–1 in the one-game final. All Canadians, including Wayne, had definitely expected a different result. Wayne was so depressed after the final game, on 13 September, that he did an unheard-of thing for him, hiding in a condominium in Florida for several days without informing even his parents of his whereabouts. He felt that he had let his country down, and that he would have to prove himself yet again during the upcoming 1981–82 season.

"A Year Like You Wouldn't Believe"

Outstanding as Wayne's first two seasons were, the third was even more so. One brief summary of his 1981–82 season, by Gretzky biographers Joseph Romain and James Duplacey, reads:

> Gretzky set a plethora of new scoring marks: 50 goals in 39 games, 10 games with at least three goals, 92 goals on the season, a new assists mark and an unheard-of 212 points total. It was an awesome display of sporting prowess, which brought him to the forefront of attention in Canada and eventually to the covers of *Time* magazine and *Sports Illustrated* in the United States.

Wayne had decided before the season began that he would try to shoot more, and this proved to be an effective strategy. By the 14th game of the new season, he had 15 goals and 14 assists, and the pace never let up, despite the occasional slowdown. In his assessment, Terry Jones calls it simply "The Greatest Single Season in Hockey History."

When Wayne hit the 50-goal mark in 39 games, on 30 December 1981, in a home game against the Philadelphia Flyers, he shattered Maurice Richard's mark of 50 goals in 50 games, set during the 1944–45 season, which had survived until Mike Bossy of the New York Islanders had equalled it in the 1979–80 season. With the Oilers leading 6–5, Wayne scored (his fifth goal of the game) into an empty net (the Flyers having pulled their goalie for an extra forward in an attempt to equalize) with only three seconds left to play.

Wayne turned 21 on 26 January 1982, in St. Louis, during an Oilers's road trip. His birthday present from team owner Peter Pocklington was a new contract worth approximately $1 million per year, and included "a shopping centre in Western Canada" that would become Wayne's property in 1988. (Walter Gretzky reports that this turned out to be an apartment block in Yellowknife.) Wayne was now the youngest superstar millionaire in sport, and attracting more attention than ever. In his Gretzky biography, Jim Benagh lists some of the ways in which Wayne's life was changing:

> People were getting to see him more often. He was in large demand to do commercials — for blue jeans, other clothes, cars, all sorts of products and hockey equipment. Authors were digging up material to write books about him. In Canada, 13 songs were written about "The Great Gretzky". He was meeting movie stars such as Goldie Hawn and Burt Reynolds. *The Sporting News* named him athlete of the year for 1981.

The commercial selling of Wayne Gretzky had begun in earnest in the summer of 1980; by the following year, a business/ marketing manager in Edmonton, Michael Barnett, was hired to assist agent Gus Badali, who was operating in Toronto. This led to the formation of Sierra Sports Group, which soon had Wayne's name associated with a life-insurance company, a men's cologne, a sportswear company, a video game, a doll, wallpaper, and lunchboxes. Altogether, Wayne's endorsements were now worth about $2 million, and other contracts were in the works. However, some offers were refused: Badali and Barnett were careful to cultivate a proper image for Wayne and avoided deals with liquor or cigarette companies.

Wayne calls 1982 the year he lost his privacy. As he closed in on Phil Esposito's NHL record of 76 goals in a single season, it became impossible for him to accede to all the requests for interviews and public appearances. His father was of the opinion that the demands on his son were wearing him down, and

37

Oilers's coach Glen Sather had to limit access to his superstar. The "Gretzky Watch" included John Zeigler, president of the NHL, and Esposito himself, who was on hand to watch Wayne equal his record against the Detroit Red Wings in game 63 of the regular schedule. Before the next game in Buffalo, Wayne escaped the media circus to visit his grandmother in Brantford, drop in at his old school, and watch his brother Keith play in a minor-league hockey game. Then, on 24 February 1982, against the Buffalo Sabres, he scored not only goal number 77, but numbers 78 and 79 as well. He would go on to score an unprecedented total of 92 goals for the regular season, which remains the NHL record.

When Wayne had 199 points with only five games left on the schedule, he persuaded his parents to fly to Calgary to watch his next game there against the Flames, when he hoped to become the first player to score 200 points in the regular season. They were not disappointed, as he notched two goals and two assists that night. He finished the season with an incredible 212 points, another record, which stood until he eclipsed it himself four years later.

Play-off Blues

In the 1981 draft, the Oilers had acquired Grant Fuhr, whom Wayne later described as the best goaltender who had ever lived. An old adage in hockey has it that great goaltending is essential for success, and particularly for fulfilling any Stanley Cup ambitions. With Andy Moog and Grant Fuhr, the Oilers were acknowledged to have probably the best goaltending duo in the NHL. Walter Gretzky also believed that if the media hadn't been so busy watching Number 99 during the 1981–82 season, they would have been raving over rugged Mark Messier (who scored 50 goals), or Paul Coffey (89 points), or Glenn Anderson (105 points), or Jari Kurri (32 goals and 86 points). After Wayne had registered his record 203rd point against the Calgary Flames, the Oilers became the first NHL team ever to score 400 goals in a season, with their victory over the Colorado Rockies in the next game. The goal was scored by right-winger Dave Lumley, who earlier in the season had threatened the NHL goals-in-consecutive-games record with a total of 12. The Oilers finished the regular season with 417 goals and 111 points, good enough for first place in the Smythe Division and second place in the league overall, and they went into the play-offs with a great deal of optimism.

The Oilers's first-round opponents were the Los Angeles Kings, a team low in the league standings, which the Oilers had beaten 6–2 and 7–3 in their last two meetings. However, the Kings won the best-of-five series; if Wayne hadn't scored a sudden-death overtime goal in game two, the Oilers might have been ousted in three straight games. In game three, they were leading 5–0 — and lost 6–5 in overtime! Obviously, the Oilers were still lacking something as a team, and the media let them know it, calling them "weak-kneed wimps" who had performed "the biggest choke in Stanley Cup history." Immediately afterwards, Wayne and Kevin Lowe obtained some respite by accepting an invitation to play for Team Canada at the World Championships in Finland. But there, too, things did not go well for the team, or for Wayne.

There was a short but happier interlude for a week in July, when the entire Gretzky clan, as well as Wayne's girlfriend Vikki Moss and her mother, accompanied Wayne and a film crew to Moscow to shoot a one-hour television special for a Winnipeg-based company. Such diversions aside, however, the off-season was long and uncomfortable for Wayne, who felt that "the calendar couldn't fly by fast enough." Until he led the Oilers to a Stanley Cup victory, and helped Canada to attain international success, his career would be unfulfilled and subject to criticism. The various individual awards — including being named Sportsman of the Year for 1982 by *Sports Illustrated* — could never compensate for his unrealized ambitions, or for others' expectations of him.

THE STANLEY CUP YEARS

To have his name engraved on the Stanley Cup is the ambition of every professional hockey player in North America, a dream that begins in boyhood, and stays until it is either achieved or sadly accepted as out of reach. It has been unattainable even for some of the greatest hockey players in the NHL, including Marcel Dionne, Gilbert Perrault, and Brad Park. At the beginning of the 1982–83 season, many people were beginning to wonder whether Wayne Gretzky's name would ever appear on the Stanley Cup, including Wayne himself.

By the end of the 1982–83 regular season, the Edmonton Oilers had scored a record 424 goals, registered 1,129 assists, and set a league record for having the most 40-plus goal-scorers in one team, with four. Wayne had won his third Art Ross Trophy in a row, among other awards, and again led his teammates confidently into the play-offs. This time the Oilers were spectacular in early postseason play, starting by defeating the Winnipeg Jets in three straight games. In the quarterfinals, against the Calgary Flames, the Oilers scored 36 goals in five games; in the semifinals, they steamrollered over the Chicago Black Hawks, four games to none. As Joseph Romain and James Duplacey put it in their Gretzky biography, Wayne "was running on high-test fuel, scoring a dozen goals and assisting on 22 others in only 12 games."

Unfortunately, it was a different story in the finals, where the three-time Stanley Cup-champion New York Islanders defeated the Oilers in four straight games, scoring 17 goals to only 6 by the Edmonton team. Wayne contributed no goals and only four assists (missing the third period of game two courtesy of a slash from Billy Smith, the Islanders' goaltender). Once more, the high hopes of the young, brash brigade from Edmonton were dashed, and another long summer of inevitable questions loomed ahead.

However, Wayne was so busy during the off-season that he couldn't brood upon the Oilers's misfortune; his time was taken up with growing business commitments, charity work, visiting his family, and rest and relaxation. He enjoyed living in Edmonton, playing golf and squash to keep fit. Kevin Lowe had moved to share a house with Mark Messier, and Wayne now lived in a penthouse suite in an exclusive apartment building overlooking the Victoria Golf Course.

The First Stanley Cup, 1984

Wayne was named captain of the Oilers before the start of the 1983–84 season. Leading by example, he went on a record scoring streak, marking 61 goals and 92 assists in only 51 games, for an average of three points a game. Then he sat out the next six games, to rest an injured shoulder that had been bothering him since early in the season! He finished the regular season with 87 goals, 118 assists, and more awards. The Oilers had a record three 50-goal scorers, with Glenn Anderson (54) and Jari Kurri (52) joining Wayne; and Paul Coffey (40) and Mark Messier (37) also contributed significantly. The Oilers finished first in the league standings, with an impressive 57–18–5 record, and the team scored 446 goals, still an NHL record.

For Wayne, however, there was a sour note during the regular season. After the Oilers had defeated the New Jersey Devils 13–4, he made some unflattering comments about his opponents which included the phrase "a Mickey Mouse operation." On his next visit there he was faced with a barrage of catcalls from fans wearing Mickey Mouse T-shirts and holding up placards bearing their uncomplimentary opinion of him. Wayne learned his lesson, and has been more circumspect in his comments about opponents ever since.

The Edmonton Oilers were more wary, too, as they entered the play-offs with high hopes yet again. They easily got by the Winnipeg Jets in the first round, but needed seven games to eliminate the stubborn Calgary Flames, before sweeping the Minnesota North Stars in four. Once more, they were in the finals against the New York Islanders, whose "Drive for Five" motivation was matched against the Oilers's "Run for One." A 1–0 victory in Long Island on a Kevin McClelland goal, backed by great goaltending from Grant Fuhr, gave the Oilers the start they needed. They lost the next game 6–1, only to rebound in dramatic fashion by winning the third game at home 7–2. However, Wayne hadn't scored a goal in 10 straight games (regular season and play-offs) against the Islanders, and a familiar critical refrain was voiced in some quarters. Then he scored the opening goal in game four, and another, and the Oilers went on to win, again by a score of 7–2, and take a lead of three games to one in the series. One more victory at home, and the Stanley Cup would be theirs — Wayne's lifelong ambition would be realized.

That victory came on 19 May 1984, by a 5–2 score, with Wayne scoring the first two goals and adding an assist on the third goal by Ken Linseman. In 19 play-off games, he had scored a total of 13 goals and assisted on 21 others. But more important than any statistics was the name "Wayne Gretzky" finally engraved on the Stanley Cup.

The sellout crowd at Northlands Coliseum was jubilant for some time after the game ended, pouring streamers and balloons down on the ice. Smiles mixed with happy tears as players skated around taking turns to hold the Cup aloft to the cheers of the fans, many of them dancing in the aisles. Mark Messier, the local boy with a family hockey tradition, was very emotional, as was Grant Fuhr, the first black player to have his name engraved on the Cup. Kevin Lowe called his mother down to the ice. But then, who wasn't emotional? Certainly not Peter Pocklington, the entrepreneur most responsible for bringing NHL hockey to Edmonton, who could now savour the fruit of his investment. And Glen Sather was enjoying the pinnacle of ambition of every coach in the league.

But the most enduring image for many was that of a constantly smiling Wayne Gretzky, alternately embracing and displaying his sport's most venerable trophy, celebrating his vindication and destiny. For that Saturday night Wayne's entire family had come to Edmonton in anticipation: his parents, sister Kim, and brothers Keith, Glen, and Brent. For a while as he skated happily around, he had Brent draped over his shoulders. In the dressing room, Walter and Phyllis Gretzky were soon drenched with champagne as they shared in their son's success, before leaving the pandemonium and allowing Wayne to continue the celebrations with his teammates and younger

FIGURE 5

Edmonton Oilers, Stanley Cup Champions, 1983–84 season.

friends. Walter writes, "He's had a lot of big moments in his career, a lot of personal triumphs and awards, but I'd never seen the look of pure joy that was on his face just then — a face streaked with sweat, champagne and tears." Six years later, when his career could boast many other achievements and milestones, Wayne wrote, "I've held women and babies and jewels and money, but nothing will ever feel as good as holding that Cup."

Mark Messier won the Conn Smythe Trophy, awarded to "the most valuable player for his team in the play-offs," in 1984. It was a tribute that Wayne warmly endorsed. "Mess" promised to be another star for the Oilers, a team already blessed with considerable — and now proven — talent. The Great One plus a great team was to equal a great future, and there was understandable talk of a dynasty in the making for the new Stanley Cup champions.

For several days after their victory, the Stanley Cup was paraded by the Oilers all over Edmonton. The players took it to their homes, to friends' businesses, to schools and hospitals, and to their favourite bars and restaurants. Many surprised but grateful Edmontonians had their photograph taken alongside "Lord Stanley's mug."

Wayne now faced an even busier off-season than ever as the proud possessor of a Stanley Cup ring, but also a more enjoyable one. Whether he was on holiday at home in Brantford or elsewhere, playing in charity sports tournaments, out with girlfriend Vikki, or following up on endorsements and business deals, the pressure was finally off. Yet even now there was another challenge looming, as he was selected to play in his second Canada Cup tournament. This time, in September, along with teammates Paul Coffey and Grant Fuhr, Wayne helped Canada to defeat the Soviets 3–2 before going on to beat Sweden in the two-game final. Once again Wayne was the individual scoring leader, with 12 points. But there was little time to rest on his laurels before the Oilers began their defence of the Stanley Cup. Now other teams would be more motivated to play against them, just as the Oilers used to be for the Islanders.

44

FIGURE 6

Ambition achieved: Wayne holds the Stanley Cup at last.

FIGURE 7

*Wayne celebrates his first Stanley Cup win with
parents, brothers, girlfriend, and friends.*

More Stanley Cups and Individual Honours

Wayne excelled over the next few years. His individual statistics, which earlier had defied belief, were now becoming commonplace as he set about beating his own and other players's records. He finished the 1984–85 season with 73 goals and 135 assists, for 208 points. Once again, the Oilers won the Stanley Cup, defeating the Philadelphia Flyers by four games to one; this time, Wayne won his first Conn Smythe Trophy — to go with his fifth Art Ross Trophy and his sixth Hart Trophy. He also picked up his first of three consecutive Chrysler-Dodge NHL Performer of the Year awards. With Captain Wayne in his prime, and with two Stanley Cup banners now hanging from the rafters of Northlands Coliseum, talk of a new NHL dynasty in Edmonton increased.

The Oilers dominated the league again during the 1985–86 season, taking first place overall with 56 wins and 119 points. Wayne scored "only" 52 goals, his lowest total in five years, but amassed an astounding 163 assists, for a new points-scoring record of 215, still the highest ever recorded in the NHL. And this was his fourth season with over 200 points, an achievement that had hockey fans everywhere shaking their heads. Wayne also took home two favourite trophies, the Art Ross and the Hart, and hoped to lead his team to its third straight Stanley Cup.

After defeating the Vancouver Canucks easily in the first round of the play-offs, the Oilers faced the Calgary Flames, a team they had dominated during the regular season. This "Battle of Alberta," however, went to a seventh and deciding game in Edmonton. Calgary took a 2–0 lead and Edmonton came back to tie; midway through the third period, an error by Oilers's defenceman Steve Smith decided the issue in the Flames' favour.

Two Stanley Cups were not regarded as nearly sufficient for a team with the Oilers's talent, and Wayne now faced the challenge of helping the team reach its potential. But he was also having to deal with a growing personal problem, which few fans knew about.

The NHL schedule of 80 games plus play-offs, in cities scattered across the North American continent, would be simply impossible without the jet airplane. It is only the ability to travel at over 500 miles per hour that enables teams to play, for example, in Los Angeles, Edmonton, Montreal, and New York, in one week. Consequently, NHL players nowadays are among the most frequent of flyers, and are prone to the modern malady known as jet lag. A few of them also suffer from a very real fear of being airborne, and Wayne Gretzky was "perhaps the most famous white-knuckle flyer in Canadian sport history," according to the *Edmonton Journal*.

Wayne says in his autobiography that his fear of flying was at its worst around 1985, but that it really started when he was 15 years old and playing Junior A hockey in the Soo. The team was constantly taking long flights in "rickety little DC-3s," and he recounts a few frightening incidents. It got worse with the Edmonton Oilers, when he sat next to the team's play-by-play TV announcer, who was an even more nervous flyer. Kevin Lowe believes that Wayne's aversion to flying is actually paranoia, and that outsiders don't realize "the depth of his anguish." Wayne documents the various treatments he tried, such as hypnotherapy and mind-control classes, some of which were more helpful than others. On Canadian airlines (the practice is not allowed on American airlines), he sometimes sits in the pilot's cabin, and this has a relaxing effect. Wayne's accomplishments on the ground are even more remarkable when his personal problem in the air is taken into account.

The biggest motivations for the Oilers organization at the beginning of the 1986–87 season were revenge against the Calgary Flames, answering the "choke" charge, and winning another Stanley Cup. The Oilers again finished first in the league (helped considerably by Wayne's 62 goals and 121 assists), but they didn't meet Calgary in the play-offs, as the Flames were eliminated in the first round by the Winnipeg Jets. Meanwhile, the Oilers got by the Los Angeles Kings, the Winnipeg Jets, and the Detroit Red Wings, to be matched against the Philadelphia Flyers in a repeat of the 1985 final. Edmonton took a two-game lead in the series, with Wayne opening the scoring in each of the first two contests, and then lost game three. After taking a 3–1 lead in games with a 4–1 win at the Spectrum, the Oilers then blew leads in games five and six to force a seventh game at the Coliseum. With the score tied at 1–1, Wayne passed to his favourite target, Jari Kurri, who scored the Cup-winning goal. Amid the hoopla and celebrations on ice afterwards, Wayne immediately sought out Steve Smith, the previous year's scapegoat, and handed him the Stanley Cup to hold aloft. The Oilers were back on track. Wayne could look forward to an enjoyable off-season, albeit another brief one: practice would soon begin for the third Canada Cup tournament, to be played in August.

If all was well in Wayne's hockey world, however, by this time his long-standing relationship with Vikki Moss was showing signs of serious strain. Their lives had been intertwined in several ways. For years, Wayne had been a close friend and big brother to Vikki's brother Joey, who has Down's syndrome, and had obtained a job for him in the Oilers's locker room. Vikki's mother, Sophie, was a one-woman public-relations department for Wayne, answering an average of 1,200 letters a month. By 1987, however, Wayne's hockey career, burgeoning business interests, and constant travel, combined with Vikki's determined pursuit of her own singing career, meant that the couple was spending a lot of time apart. Vikki had moved to Los Angeles to further her career, and resisted Wayne's requests for her to return to Edmonton and get married.

Ironically, it was in Los Angeles, very soon afterwards, that a disconsolate Wayne found solace, when he ran into Janet Jones at a Lakers basketball game. They had been casual acquaintances for years, but this meeting, in May of 1987, was to change both their lives. Janet was a successful actress, dancer, and model, who had recently ended a two-year engagement to tennis star Vitas Gerulaitis.

New Love and Old Rivalry

Wayne was thoroughly smitten, and he spent as much time as possible with Janet. A couple of weeks together in Los Angeles,

FIGURE 8

A familiar sight: Wayne scores against the Boston Bruins.

FIGURE 9

*A sense of déjà vu: Wayne and Gordie Howe reenact
their 1972 pose in the Oilers's dressing room.*

for example, were followed by another at Paul Coffey's cottage in the wilderness of northern Ontario. Around this time, too, Wayne was seriously contemplating retirement from hockey, saying that he was mentally and physically exhausted. Hockey had been his main focus since he was six years old, and the pressures were multiplying with each new challenge. In fact, he delayed accepting an invitation to play in Rendezvous '87 for two months, until his father persuaded him that he had to play for his country. When he did report for training camp, in August, Janet went along as well (taking the opportunity to visit Wayne's family in Brantford), and their relationship became public knowledge. Some were unhappy about the fact that Wayne was dating an American woman (weren't Canadian women good enough for the Great One?) — and one who had appeared in the March 1987 issue of *Playboy* magazine — but nothing could mar the couple's happiness.

The 1987 Canada Cup tournament provided a thrilling three-game final between Canada and the USSR, each game ending in a 6–5 score. As well, Mario Lemieux, Number 66 of the Pittsburgh Penguins, often touted as the NHL's next superstar, was playing alongside Number 99. They worked well together: Lemieux scored the winning goal with only 1:25 remaining in the final game, on a set-up from Wayne. For the third time in a row in this tournament, Wayne finished up as scoring leader, with 21 points.

Now Wayne was expected to lead the Oilers to their fourth Stanley Cup, at a time when he wanted to spend as much time with Janet as possible. Obviously, 1988 promised to be interesting in more ways than one, but no one could have predicted just how interesting.

WEDDING VOWS AND
THE GREAT TRADE

Despite their success, the Edmonton Oilers were not a completely happy group of campers at the beginning of the 1987–88 season. In November, disgruntled all-star defenceman Paul

Coffey was traded to Pittsburgh (in exchange for Craig Simpson, who became a 50-goal scorer for the Oilers). Wayne was also having some doubts about his contract with Pocklington, and was unhappy with some aspects of Sather's coaching style. On 30 December, playing against the Philadelphia Flyers, he sustained a knee injury that kept him sidelined until February. In January, during the enforced rest period and while Janet was away in South Carolina, a pining Wayne bought a diamond ring, proposed by telephone, and was accepted. The engagement was announced and the wedding set for 16 July in Edmonton.

On 19 February, in a game against the Pittsburgh Penguins, Wayne suffered a corneal abrasion and hemorrhaging behind the left eye, courtesy of an errant stick, which gave him another week's rest. Then, on March 1st, playing against the L.A. Kings at Northlands Coliseum, he made more hockey history by breaking one of the NHL's most revered records: Gordie Howe's lifetime assist mark of 1,049. But whereas his hero had needed 1,767 games to amass that total, Wayne had got there in only 681 games. The game was halted while he received a Tiffany-crafted clock from the NHL; and a golden hockey stick and a $50,000 bond payable upon his first child's 21st birthday.

Wayne went on to lead the league in assists for the ninth straight year, but, because he missed 16 games, he had his first NHL season with fewer than 50 goals. No matter, however, as he outdid himself in the play-offs. The Oilers first beat the Winnipeg Jets in five tough games, then faced Calgary, which had finished first in the league, in the next round. After a 3–1 Oilers win at the Saddledome in game one, on 19 April, Wayne received a telephone call from Janet in Edmonton, telling him that she was pregnant. The expectant father celebrated by scoring a shorthanded, overtime, winning goal in game two, a goal he rates as his biggest NHL goal ever. The Flames lost the next two games, and the Oilers went on to beat the Detroit Red Wings in five games, which put them in their fifth Stanley Cup finals in six years, this time against the Boston Bruins.

In game five of the series, with the score tied 3–3 and three minutes left in the second period, the lights suddenly went out in Boston Gardens. The game had to be cancelled, and it was rescheduled in Edmonton, where the Oilers clinched their fourth Stanley Cup with a 6–3 victory. With 43 points in 19 play-off games, Wayne set more new records, and was a shoo-in for his second Conn Smythe Trophy.

The Great Wedding

As the date of Wayne and Janet's wedding, 16 July 1988, drew nearer, the media barrage became so overwhelming that the couple sometimes regretted their decision to marry in Edmonton. On the cover of the 25 July 1988 issue of *Maclean's*, Wayne and his bride were featured under the title "The Royal Wedding," and there was a six-page story inside. *Maclean's* described the wedding as "the union of a talented and gentlemanly sports hero who, for many Canadians, embodies some of the nation's most cherished values, and his glamorous American princess."

About 700 guests attended the ceremony at Edmonton's Roman Catholic cathedral, including relatives and friends of both families and celebrities from the entertainment and sports worlds. Two of the special guests were Wayne's idol, Gordie Howe, and his Soviet friend, goalie Vladislav Tretiak. The streets outside the church were lined with thousands of well-wishers when the happy couple emerged on the steps. After a reception presided over by Alan Thicke, which Wayne described as "a gas," the newlyweds retired for the night to the Westin Hotel's Crown Suite.

Wayne and Janet went south to Janet's apartment in Los Angeles, where they intended to spend the summer. But they didn't have much time together, for instance, to go for a drive, either in the new Rolls Royce he had given her for a wedding present, or in his own custom champagne-coloured Nissan 300zx convertible, before they were involved again in headlines of a much different sort. Less than a month after their wedding came the shocking news that Wayne was being traded.

FIGURE 10

*Mess, Gretz, and Kevin celebrate their last
Stanley Cup together, May 1988.*

The Great Trade

Some dissension had surfaced within the Oilers organization long before Wayne's wedding, and his relationship with his employers was not without some tension. Still, he and Janet were planning to buy a house and settle in Edmonton, information that they passed on to Walter Gretzky during a celebration dinner only hours after the Oilers won the Stanley Cup in May 1988. Consequently, Wayne was quite surprised when his father reluctantly told him of well-founded rumours that owner Peter Pocklington had been trying to trade him.

The news could not have come as a total shock, however. Wayne's personal-service contract with Pocklington would allow him to leave in five years as an unrestricted free agent, a potentially tremendous career advantage to look forward to, and the owner had made no progress in efforts to sign him to an extension. Complicating the issue further was the fact that Pocklington's many other business interests were failing, to the extent that the Oilers had been put up as collateral against a large loan from the Alberta government. One solution to the financial impasse would be for Pocklington to sell his 27-year-old superstar now, for full value, rather than take whatever he could get five years down the road.

While Wayne was still on his honeymoon, Bruce McNall, owner of the Los Angeles Kings, telephoned to say that he had permission to talk to him about a possible trade. Wayne was annoyed not to have received any previous indication of this from the Oilers organization, but was receptive to the idea. If he was to go anywhere, Los Angeles offered the possibility of Janet resuming her Hollywood career, a larger market for potential off-ice endorsements, and the challenge of helping to sell hockey in an American city not noted for its devotion to the sport. In addition, he had many friends in the area, several of them celebrities in show business and sports. He was already acquainted with Bruce McNall, too, and liked him. After some difficult and unpleasant negotiations with Pocklington, a deal was eventually reached between the parties in late July, although it would not be consummated until two weeks later.

What was described as "the Trade of the Century" was settled

FIGURE 11

The Great Wedding, 16 July 1988.

early on Tuesday, 9 August, when the Edmonton Oilers sent Wayne, and forwards Mike Krushelnyski and Marty McSorley to the L.A. Kings in exchange for forwards Jimmy Carson and Martin Gélinas; the Kings's first-round draft picks in 1989, 1991, and 1993; and $15 million in cash. As Gretzky biographer Stephen Hanks put it, it appeared that "Los Angeles [had] traded much of their future for a chance to have The Great One add a Stanley Cup to their present." Once the details were made public, reaction was swift; television programming was interrupted across North America to announce the trade. The news dominated the next day's headlines, and set off a ferocious debate, particularly across Canada. The entire front page of the 12 August 1988 edition of the *Edmonton Journal*, under the banner headline "Gretzky Gone," was devoted to the news, as were the daily editorial ("Hockey's gain is city's loss"), the opinion-page daily cartoon (Pocklington in a booth at Northlands Coliseum vainly trying to sell season tickets with his superstar gone), and several pages of the sports section. At the press conference following the trade, Wayne declined to read a prepared statement and said, "I decided that for the benefit of myself, my new wife and our expected child . . . it would be beneficial to let me play for the Los Angeles Kings." He was unable to conclude his spontaneous remarks without choking back the tears at several points, and eventually he couldn't go on.

Vancouver sports columnist Jim Taylor, coauthor with Wayne's father of the book *Gretzky* published four years earlier, probably expressed the sentiments of many Canadians when he wrote in *Sports Illustrated*, under the title "A Nation in Mourning":

Forget the controversy over whether No. 99 jumped or was pushed; the best hockey player in the world was ours, and the Americans flew up from Hollywood in their private jet and bought him. It wasn't the Canadian heart that was torn, it was the Canadian psyche that was ripped by an uppercut to the paranoia. . . . In the minds of Edmontonians and Canadian hockey fans everywhere, Gretzky had been theirs to keep.

Wayne's teammates in the Oilers were upset, even though they were in a better position than anyone to understand that hockey is a business, one in which the players are merely well-paid employees. A predictable blast came from Pittsburgh, where ex-Oiler Paul Coffey charged that his friend "Gretz" had been traded "like a piece of meat." Pleas were even made to the Canadian government to prevent the trade. But the anger and dismay were most vehement, obvious, and long-lasting in Edmonton, among thousands of loyal Oilers's fans who felt betrayed and disgusted.

Wayne's pregnant wife became an immediate target of blame for many. In their view, the trade confirmed the fact that Janet had forced Wayne to leave Canada, so soon after their wedding, so that she could resume her Hollywood career. She was called "Jezebel Janet," "dragon lady," and "witch." Some did come to her defence, giving her credit for Wayne's newfound happiness, but she shed a few tears over the criticism and, according to her husband, still bears the scars.

However, more wrath was directed at the man who had sold Wayne and pocketed $15 million in the process, Oilers owner Peter Pocklington. An entrepreneurial hero for bringing an NHL franchise to Edmonton, he was suddenly cast in the role of villain. He was hanged in effigy outside of the Northlands Coliseum, and hockey fans threatened to boycott the meat and dairy products of the companies he owned. Pocklington retaliated by making some uncomplimentary remarks about the size of Wayne's ego and his acting ability at the press conference, and said that he could have backed out of the deal up to the moment he made his public statement. Janet joined the fray in her husband's defence to dispute Pocklington's claims, saying that he was the reason Wayne was no longer an Edmonton Oiler. A few months later, Wayne was quoted in the February 1989 issue of *Esquire* magazine:

And I hear that he says I faked the tears. I was the most pissed off I've ever been at a person in my whole life. Over the past ten years, I had played in every exhibition game and never missed a promotional appearance. I had done everything he'd ever asked me to do, and we'd won four

FIGURE 12

Tears at the press conference after
the Great Trade, 9 August 1988.

*A city shows its gratitude: The Wayne Gretzky statue
outside the Northlands Coliseum, Edmonton.*

Stanley Cups. For him to throw all that away with one silly remark didn't make any sense.

The full inside story of the deal may never be known. In his 1990 Gretzky biography, Stephen Hanks states that the truth probably lies somewhere between Pocklington's version of events and Wayne's interpretation. Joseph Romain and James Duplacey write in their 1992 biography, "Almost nobody bought the Pocklington/Gretzky version of events," since both parties eventually benefited so much from the deal. We may never know, but there were some certainties for Canadian hockey fans: Wayne's tears were real, he was indeed gone, and the Los Angeles Kings were now a vastly improved team. Their reaction was probably summed up best by journalist Jim Taylor: "If this be free trade, stuff it."

LIFE IN LOS ANGELES

Wayne's reception in Los Angeles was little short of phenomenal. Fans of the lowly L.A. Kings had visions of future Stanley Cups with the Great One aboard. Some businessmen drooled over the profit potential of Wayne Gretzky in their bigger market, and the merchandising of L.A. Kings souvenirs and trinkets was rejuvenated overnight. Season ticket sales in the Great Western Forum more than doubled, despite higher prices, with such Hollywood luminaries as Milton Berle, the Pointer Sisters, and Sylvester Stallone among the purchasers. In short, according to Gretzky biographers Romain and Duplacey, "Wayne was wined and dined, hosted and toasted by the who's who of Tinseltown . . . [and] hockey became almost de rigeur [sic] among the Gucci crowd." Back in Brantford, Wayne's parents had resisted all their son's efforts to buy them an upscale residence, preferring to remain in their modest home on Varadi Avenue. But on the very day that Wayne was traded, 9 August, workers came to install a swimming pool in the backyard, courtesy of Wayne and Janet, where the "Wally Coliseum" had first been flooded 23 years before. Meanwhile, the younger Gretzkys moved into a luxurious six-bedroom home in Encino, California. If Edmonton had been the right place before, Los Angeles certainly seemed the place to be now.

Peculiar Salary Negotiations

The amicable and personal nature of the salary negotiations between Wayne and future boss Bruce McNall in the summer of 1988, conducted on a flight from Edmonton to L.A., were peculiar to say the least — and the result had a lasting effect upon the NHL's salary structure. Wayne's version of their conversation matches almost exactly McNall's account, which is quoted at length in the 1992 book *Net Worth: Exploding the Myths of Pro Hockey*, by David Cruise and Alison Griffiths. (One should bear in mind, too, that McNall was voluntarily renegotiating the contract Wayne had with the Oilers, after paying Pocklington for one player nearly the amount he had paid for the whole L.A. Kings franchise.) According to McNall,

> "I said, 'Wayne, I have to be honest with you. . . . I know basically what most players in this League should be making, but I have no idea in your case. I have no idea.' He said, 'Well, I don't either.' So I threw out a number to him [$3 million a year]. I said, 'How does this sound?' He goes, 'No, no, that's way too much. How about this amount' [$1 million]. I said, 'I don't think that is consistent with what will happen in the near future. We don't want to have to redo this every two minutes.'
>
> "So we were negotiating in reverse. He was at one price lower and I was trying to pull him up. He was trying to keep it down. That was before we ever sold a ticket. That was before we ever knew his value to the franchise. He could have said '$10 million a year is what I want.' "

Eventually, they settled on $2.5 million (American) a year, in an eight-year contract that also involved some team bonuses and incentives — and apparently a promise from McNall, sealed

63

with a handshake, that no other hockey player would ever earn more than Wayne.

A look at some of the ensuing financial ramifications, during the period in which the Bruce-and-Wayne union was evolving into a partnership of sorts, reveals just how astute McNall had been. Before Wayne went to Los Angeles, attendance at Inglewood was hovering around the 10,000 mark, bringing around $4 million in gate receipts for the Kings. These jumped to $13 million for the 1989–90 season, and McNall believes that Wayne added another $15 million in advertising revenues and improved the Kings's cash flow to between $7 million and $10 million a year, and that by 1991 the franchise was worth approximately $100 million, or five times as much as it had been before Wayne's arrival!

King Gretzky

In their seven seasons in the Smythe Division of the NHL before Wayne joined the team, the L.A. Kings had never finished higher than fourth place. They had managed to reach the division final in the play-offs only once, in 1982, when they lost to the Vancouver Canucks in five games. So when Wayne skated onto the ice for his first game in the Kings's new-look black-and-silver uniform, there was certainly room for improvement, and the opening-night crowd at the Great Western Forum was expecting the Great One to provide it. The game against the Detroit Red Wings was the first sellout for a home opener in the Kings's 22-year history. His presence had made hockey chic in L.A., and now the fans expected him to make it successful as well.

Wayne did not disappoint, scoring a goal with his first shot, and adding three assists, as the Kings easily defeated the Red Wings 8–2. The Kings went on to win their first four games, in fact, off to their best start ever. Although Wayne did not have the superlative supporting cast that he had enjoyed in Edmonton, the Kings did have some potential; several talented players were now delighted to be playing with him and were responding to his leadership. Offence was the team's strongest suit. The team's big scorer before Wayne's arrival had been third-year left-winger Luc Robitaille, who had marked 53 goals and 58 assists (111 points) for fifth place in the NHL scoring race the previous season, and had earned the 1987 NHL Rookie-of-the-Year honours. Eight-year veteran centre Bernie Nicholls had scored 32 goals and added 46 assists in the 1987–88 season, and other veterans Dave Taylor (67 points) and Bobby Carpenter (52 points) had contributed significantly as well. More experience had just been added up front, with the signing of free agent John Tonelli, late of the Calgary Flames and New York Islanders. On defence, the Kings were less impressive but still respectable, with Steve Duchesne (55 points) leading the way. Ex-Oiler Marty McSorley had accompanied Wayne in the trade (at Wayne's insistence); he was a rugged defenceman who could be relied upon to protect Wayne whenever necessary, as Dave Semenko had done in Edmonton. All NHL teams had such "tough guys" in their lineup, variously referred to as "enforcers," "police-men," or even "goons," to prevent opponents from taking liberties with any of their smaller, more skilful teammates. The Kings's goaltending was acknowledged to be unreliable, how-ever, and their penalty killing had been weak. The coach was 36-year-old Robbie Ftorek, who had joined the team only mid-way through the 1987–88 season.

Still, at training camp, Wayne was of the opinion that the Kings were a well-balanced team that should have a successful season and be a contender in the play-offs. But always in his mind at the beginning of the 1988–89 season was a certain date on the calendar, the first time that he would return to Edmon-ton to play against the Oilers. For obvious reasons, 19 October was a day Wayne dreaded.

Welcome Back

Wayne was apprehensive about what kind of reception he would get from the Edmonton fans and various members of the Oilers organization, and especially about having to play against some of his best friends on the Oilers. Northlands Coliseum had been sold out for months, and the game was attended by 17,503 people, the Oilers's biggest crowd ever. As well, the game was broadcast in a special midweek edition of *Hockey Night in Canada*. He needn't have worried; the fans gave a standing ovation lasting nearly four minutes when he finally skated onto the ice.

Then it was down to business. Oilers's fans were willing for Wayne to do well, as long as their team won the game. They cheered his first shift, his first touch of the puck, and his two assists — and they also cheered loudly when Mark Messier checked him against the boards. The game was a difficult one, and it was a relief when it was over, culminating in an 8–6 win for the Oilers. Besieged by reporters afterwards, still asking questions about the trade and life in Los Angeles, Wayne took the opportunity to confirm his patriotism. According to Gretzky biographer Fred McFadden, he said, "I'm still proud to be a Canadian. I didn't desert my country. I moved because I was traded and that's where my job is. But I'm Canadian to the core. I hope that all Canadians understand that." If his reception in Edmonton was anything to go by, Canadians bore him no grudge.

Once this first return trip was over, going back to Edmonton became much easier for Wayne. He certainly enjoyed his second visit to the city, in February 1989, for the all-star game, his tenth in a row, leading the Campbell Conference against the Wales Conference, which included his main rival for individual honours in the NHL, Mario Lemieux. He was happy to be reunited with former Oiler teammates Grant Fuhr, Jari Kurri, Kevin Lowe, and Mark Messier for this special occasion, put on one of his superlative displays in a 9–5 victory for his team, and was named most valuable player.

By the time Wayne played in the all-star game, the Kings had a record of 25 wins, 15 losses, and 1 tie, by far their best first half of a season in many years. Wayne was dominant on the ice, and more assertive in the locker room than he had been with the Oilers. On 23 November 1988, playing against the Detroit Red Wings, he scored his 600th career goal. On 19 December at 11:55 a.m., in Cedars-Sinai Hospital in Los Angeles, Janet gave birth to a daughter, Paulina Mary Jean. Wayne was ecstatic, and immediately stepped happily into a new role as doting father.

But he was still the Great One on the ice. The Kings finished the season with a 42–31–7 record, for second place in the Smythe Division, ahead of the third-place Oilers. In one year, they had moved from 18th place in the league to fourth, one of the biggest turnarounds in NHL history. Wayne finished with 54 goals and 114 points, good enough to win him the Hart Trophy as league MVP for a record ninth time in ten seasons. He calls it one of the most satisfactory seasons of his life, and the best was yet to come. The Kings went on to defeat the Oilers in seven games in the first round of the play-offs, after the Oilers had held a 3–1 lead in games. Again it was not easy to play against his old friends — they never spoke to each other during the series — but Wayne felt vindicated afterwards. Game seven was a 6–3 victory for the Kings, celebrated by a sellout crowd of 16,005 at the Forum. Although the Kings lost in the next round to the Calgary Flames, their supporters had tasted enough success since Wayne's arrival to be optimistic about the future.

By this time, Wayne was one of a handful of people who had been painted by both Andy Warhol and leRoy Neiman. But how many 28-year-old athletes, at the height of their powers and still performing, have a life-sized statue erected in their honour? Outside the Northlands Coliseum is one of Wayne, in his Edmonton Oilers uniform (with his jersey tucked in on one side), holding the Stanley Cup above his head.

A Special Record

Going into the 1989–90 season, Wayne was only 13 points shy of the NHL's most prestigious individual record: the all-time points mark of Gordie Howe, who had amassed 1,850 points in 1,767 games. Howe and Wayne had become firm friends over the years, and Howe was on hand as Wayne approached the landmark. By the fifth game of the season, Wayne was within

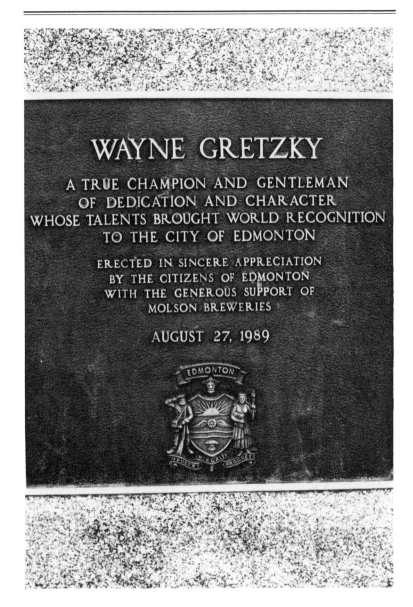

FIGURE 14

Inscription on statue.

striking distance, needing four points. In that game, against Vancouver, he assisted on three goals, to fall one short. "The Great Gretzky Tour" then moved to Edmonton for the next game, on 15 October 1989, where tickets were at a premium and hotel accommodation was scarce, as once again the media and fans flocked to the Northlands Coliseum for a historic hockey occasion.

Early in the game, Wayne assisted on a goal by Bernie Nicholls to tie the record, but from that point things became more difficult. Esa Tikkanen, the Finnish Oiler acknowledged to be the best "shadow" in the league, followed Wayne around the rink religiously, and a hit by big Oiler defenceman Jeff Beukeboom left Wayne feeling dizzy for a spell. Goals were being scored by both teams, but Wayne was not getting any more points. With 4:40 remaining in the third period, the Oilers took a 4-3 lead. Then, with only 53 seconds left in the game, Wayne scored a backhand goal for his 1,851st point — in only 780 games! The fans gave him a standing ovation, and the game was interrupted for ten minutes while he received the congratulations of family, friends, and dignitaries, as well as assorted commemorative gifts from the Kings, the Oilers, and the NHL. And after the ceremonies had concluded and the game resumed, he led the Kings to victory, by scoring the winning goal in overtime.

Play-off Blues

However, there was no fairy-tale finish to the 1989–90 season for the Kings. By January, the team was languishing in fourth place in the Smythe Division (where it eventually ended the season). Bernie Nicholls was traded to the New York Rangers for two right-wingers, Tony Granato and Tomas Sandstrom. Wayne pleaded for Nicholls to remain, but to no avail. Injuries throughout the season to several of the Kings's best players didn't help the team's fortunes. Wayne missed two games in March with a groin injury, and the final five games of the season and first two of the play-offs with a back injury. Still suffering from occasional spasms, he returned in game three to contribute to the Kings's eventual victory over the Calgary Flames in six games, which placed them in the Smythe Division final against the Edmonton Oilers.

In game four of the first round, the Kings had routed the Flames 12–4, and the Sandstrom-Gretzky-Granato line had 15 points, so they had every reason to be confident against the Oilers. But the Great Trade had created an enduring rivalry between the two clubs. Wayne wanted to win with the Kings as he had done in Edmonton; the Oilers wanted to show that they could win without him. Their respective motivations had surfaced in a game at Los Angeles on 28 February, when the Oilers, coming off a bad loss to the Flames, and the Kings, in a slump, engaged in an all-out brawl that set an NHL record for penalties. Wayne had long been identified as a proponent of removing the fighting from hockey, leaving him open to the charge that he always had others, like McSorley or Semenko, to do his fighting for him. But in the heated exchanges of 28 February, even Wayne got involved, jumping on one of the Oilers, and drawing a rare penalty.

This was the last meeting between the Kings and the Oilers before they met again in the play-offs. It was an anti-climax, to say the least. Wayne reinjured his back in game three, never returned, and the Oilers won in four straight games. They then proceeded to defeat Chicago in six games, and Boston in five, to win their fifth Stanley Cup, bringing a smile back to the faces of their fans (and to Peter Pocklington). Mark Messier won the Hart Trophy as MVP, and Wayne picked up his eighth Art Ross Trophy for his 142 points in the regular season.

The Written Word

As the 1990s began, there was no question that Wayne Gretzky had been the outstanding hockey player of the 1980s — the greatest ever, according to many experts — and the amount written about him during that decade was nothing short of phenomenal. In fact, in a poll conducted by Associated Press,

Wayne was selected as the best athlete of the 1980s, finishing ahead of such stars as Earvin "Magic" Johnson of the Lakers, Olympic track star Carl Lewis, and football player Joe Montana. As of this writing, the number of Wayne Gretzky biographies is already into double figures, and he hasn't retired yet. Edmonton sportswriter Terry Jones wrote *The Great Gretzky* in 1980, when Wayne was just 19 years old, his professional NHL hockey career just underway. Jones followed up in 1982 with a book entitled *The Great Gretzky, Yearbook II: The Greatest Single Season in Hockey History*. Three other biographies appeared in the same year: Jim Benagh's *Picture Story of Wayne Gretzky*; S.H. Burchard's *Sports Star Wayne Gretzky*; and Meguido Zola's *Gretzky! Gretzky! Gretzky!*

Two years later, the most authoritative book to date appeared, with comprehensive and inside information and insights that had never been available in print before. The timing of its publication was superb, in the stores just after the Edmonton Oilers won their first Stanley Cup, with a picture on the dust jacket of a smiling Wayne Gretzky, in a tuxedo, holding the large and venerable trophy. This was *Gretzky: From the Back Yard Rink to the Stanley Cup*, written by his father, Walter Gretzky, and Vancouver sportswriter Jim Taylor. Janet Mersky Leder's work, published in 1986, was called, simply, *Wayne Gretzky*.

Three more biographical works appeared in 1990, two of them also titled *Wayne Gretzky*, one written by Stephen Hanks and the other by Fred McFadden. The other book was Wayne's autobiography, written with the assistance of *Sports Illustrated* writer Rick Reilly. In 1991 there followed *Wayne Gretzky: Hockey Great*, by Thomas R. Raber; Joseph Romain and James Duplacey produced their book entitled *Wayne Gretzky* in 1992.

The story in every Gretzky biography is that of a large, united, and loving family, a talented son who surmounts every challenge presented to him in his career, reaches pinnacles of fame and fortune, then marries a beautiful showgirl and becomes a loving parent himself. All of these writers are unstinting in their compliments. McFadden quotes another writer on Wayne: "He seems almost too good to be true. He is not merely the best hockey player in the world, but one of the nicest and most unspoiled." Hanks, in an introductory chapter, describes Wayne "as approachable, intelligent, witty, and articulate as any athlete in pro sports." And Romain and Duplacey write, "He is polite to the press, indulgent with his fans, gives generously to social causes, and voices no political opinions. His display of virtue and clean living ranks The Great One among the most remarkable entertainment professionals of this, or any other time." Even *The Canadian Encyclopedia* waxes lyrical in its entry on Wayne: "His personal charm as well as his scoring feats have endeared him to the N[orth] American sporting public."

The 1990–91 Season

Wayne and Janet's second child, Ty Robert, was born in July of 1990, with training camp just around the corner for Wayne. At the end of the regular season, Wayne was in his familiar place at the top of the standings, amassing 21 more points than in 1989–90, and winning his ninth Art Ross Trophy. There were highlights along the way: he became the first NHL player to score 2,000 points, against the Winnipeg Jets, on 23 October 1990, and scored his 700th NHL goal, on 3 January 1991, in a 6–3 win over the New York Islanders. Gretzky watchers now began to contemplate the possibility of his reaching absolutely unheard-of plateaux in his sport — 3,000 points, or maybe even 4,000.

In the spring of 1991, there was certainly cause for optimism that the Kings could go all the way to a Stanley Cup. Under new coach Tom Webster, the Kings finished the regular season with 102 points and first place in the Smythe Division, a feat they had last accomplished 16 years before. They were third in the league overall, and 22 points ahead of those troublesome Oilers. But in the end, their hopes were frustrated again by the team from Edmonton, in a loss that was harder than usual to bear. The two teams met in the division final, Edmonton having survived a seven-game series against Calgary, and Los Angeles having taken their series in six games against Vancouver. The first three games all went into overtime, and all finished with a 4–3 score, but the Oilers won two of them. Wayne was hit by the puck in the first period of game three, and did not return; he needed 25 stitches to close the ear wound. The Kings lost the series in six games, the last game also ending in a 4–3 overtime win for the Oilers. The closeness of the series was indicated by the total goal count, with the Oilers scoring 21 to the Kings's 20.

One month later, on 30 May 1991, the Kings (with enthusiastic input from Wayne) acquired Jari Kurri. Kurri had left the Edmonton Oilers at the end of the 1989–90 season and played in Italy. He was then acquired by the Philadelphia Flyers and immediately traded to Los Angeles in a package deal with other players. During their eight seasons together with the Oilers, Wayne and Kurri had proved to be probably the best offensive tandem in NHL history, with Wayne scoring 532 goals in that span and Kurri scoring 397. So soon after their exit from the 1991 play-offs, the phrase "Wait until next year!" now had some real meaning for the Los Angeles Kings. In June, the Kings acquired, via Minnesota, another player who had been in Edmonton during those eight seasons, defenceman Charlie Huddy.

Before Wayne could play again with Jari Kurri, however, he had to play against him, in the 1991 Canada Cup Tournament. Kurri played for Finland, while Wayne was representing Canada for the fourth time in this international test of hockey supremacy. Again, he finished up as the individual scoring leader, with 12 points; Team Canada centre Mark Messier said afterwards, "I've never seen him play better." Although he was injured and had to sit out the final game against Team USA, the fans in Hamilton's Copps Coliseum showed their appreciation by chanting his name.

The crowd's loudest boos were reserved for American defenceman Gary Suter, the man who had given Wayne a hard check from behind that propelled him a few feet into the boards. Wayne had lain motionless for a while before getting to his feet, and had to be helped to the dressing room. He suffered a twisted knee and was experiencing back spasms, thought to be a recurrence of his injury from two seasons earlier. There was no penalty called on the play, but replays afterwards of "the hit

Captain of the Los Angeles Kings.

heard around the world" stimulated a great deal of debate. A diplomatic Wayne helped to cool passions by saying that, in his opinion, it was a legal hit, and that Suter had not intentionally tried to hurt him. Suter agreed, adding that if it had been anyone else except Wayne Gretzky "we wouldn't be talking about it."

Endorsements and Investments

On the other hand, Wayne's life off the ice had never been so prosperous. His positive feelings toward his new employer at the time of the Great Trade were soon borne out in their relationship, which expanded into a genuine friendship based on mutual respect. Wayne's credentials in hockey were matched by Bruce McNall's experience and status as a successful entrepreneur. McNall had begun coin-collecting at the age of 10, developing a particular interest in ancient Greek and Roman coins, and gradually turned his lifelong hobby into a most profitable business. Ambitions to become a professor of ancient history gave way to the more lucrative career of trading coins, and he now owns Numismatic Fine Arts International in Los Angeles. McNall also became involved in other high-risk investments such as Hollywood movies, race horses, and struggling sports franchises (through McNall Sports & Entertainment).

As a young millionaire in Edmonton, Wayne had also become involved in several investments. His first venture in a sports franchise was in 1985, when he bought into the Belleville Bulls of the Ontario Hockey Association; later, he purchased the Hull Olympics of the Quebec Major Junior Hockey League. Most of the growing fortune that made such investments possible came from endorsement contracts with such major companies as American Express, General Mills, Gillette, and Nissan. By the time he arrived in Los Angeles, he was an astute businessman. In his Gretzky biography, McFadden catalogues Wayne's endorsements:

They have used his name to sell everything from lunch boxes to insurance policies. He has contracts to support

Nike shoes and sports clothes, Titan hockey sticks, Jofa helmets and hockey equipment, Daoust skates, Neilson chocolates, 7-Up soft drinks, Travellers Insurance, GWG jeans, Mattel dolls and hockey games, Pro-Stars cereal, and Coca-Cola. His name and picture have been used in a vast array of products, from wallpaper and bedsheets to telephones, watches, frisbees, and pencil boxes.

In addition, Wayne was associated with Air Canada Vacations, Canon Cameras, Easton, Lloyd's Bank of Canada, Peak, and Thrifty Car Rentals.

Wayne had made what he admitted was a forgettable acting début in the television daytime serial drama *The Young and the Restless* in 1981, but it was a learning experience and he was always a quick study; he soon displayed a more natural and convincing ability before the cameras. With his achievements in hockey and his pleasant personality, Wayne was much sought after, as evidenced by a remark in the June 1983 issue of *Advertising Age Magazine*: "If the world's leading marketers got together to invent the ideal athlete to endorse their product, anyone suggesting an athlete with the credentials and personality of Wayne Gretzky would be accused of pipe-dreaming."

Wayne has also given freely of his time to make public-service announcements for good causes, such as those with his pal Joey Moss for the Canadian Mental Health Association. And in December of 1991, Thrifty Car Rentals offered customers a copy of his autobiography in return for a donation of at least 99 cents to the Braille Literacy Foundation. This campaign accumulated $22,000, which Wayne presented to the local branch of one of his favourite charities, the Canadian National Institute for the Blind.

It is perhaps surprising, even in these days of skyrocketing incomes for sports celebrities, that in the 1992 ranking of the world's top 40 highest-paid athletes by *Forbes* magazine Wayne is ranked in only 15th place. On the other hand, he is the only hockey player on the list. In a 1991 article entitled "Gretzky Business," in *Profit* magazine, John Southerst and Rick Spence write, "Not as fast as Hull or as tough as Howe, Wayne Gretzky rewrote the NHL record book by combining talent, persistence and an entrepreneurial instinct for innovation."

By the time the *Profit* article appeared, Wayne and McNall had become business partners in several profitable enterprises, and spent a great deal of their leisure time together. There are obvious dangers in this: a player can be accused of "sucking up" to the owner, and so antagonize his teammates. The owner is vulnerable, being labelled a "jock-sniffer," who is "ass-tight" with his player. But what Gretzky biographer Terry Jones has dubbed "The Bruce and Wayne Show" was the real thing, later surviving the supreme test of the first-ever NHL players's strike.

In Edmonton, Wayne had part-ownership of a thoroughbred race horse. McNall, who owned Summa Stables, took Wayne to his first Kentucky Derby, an outing that Wayne thoroughly enjoyed. The upshot was that he and McNall invested together in some race horses, and the joint venture was very successful, adding more millions to their already swollen coffers. Their thoroughbreds, and notably Golden Pheasant, have won some prestigious races, including the Arc de Triomphe and the Arlington Million.

On the board of directors at the Hollywood Park racecourse with McNall was Harry Ornest, owner of the Toronto Argonauts of the Canadian Football League. In 1989, the Argos had been granted rights to hold their games in Toronto's new state-of-the-art facility, the Skydome. Seeing an opportunity to turn a deficit operation around there, McNall discussed the possibility with an enthusiastic Wayne, and then purchased the team in 1991 with two main partners: Wayne and comedy actor John Candy, each of whom acquired twenty percent of the franchise. The trio then demonstrated their serious intent by bringing the most sought-after American college player, Raghib "Rocket" Ismail, to the Argos for a reported $30.1 million. It was yet another successful venture: a few months later, the Toronto Argonauts won the Grey Cup.

McNall and Wayne also paid around half a million dollars for a rare 1910 baseball card of Hall-of-Fame player Honus Wagner, an item expected to double in value someday. And Wayne has paid $16,000 for a letter in which Alexander Graham Bell writes about his first phone call, from his — and Wayne's — hometown of Brantford.

WAYNE'S WORLD

Thanks to the miracle of advertising, it's like Gretz never left

PAMELA YUZDA
Special to The Journal

Edmonton

NHL 75ᵗ ANNIVERSARY COLLECTOR EDITION GLASSES

YOURS TO KEEP!
(COLLECT ALL 4 DESIGNS)

'Wayne has transcended his game like no other player. He's an ambassador for the sport and a role model for children.'

•

When it comes to deals for hockey equipment — first Titan-Jofa, now Easton — Wayne's expertise shines. But he has also smiled for Canon Cameras, Lloyd's Bank of Canada and recently began promoting car rentals for Thrifty, who in December offered customers a copy of Wayne's book Gretzky in return for a donation to The Braille Literacy Foundation.

ayne's still with us.

Though nothing's been the same since the day of The Big Trade, he's still a part of our lives.

Through the intrusiveness of advertising, Wayne enters our homes, peddling soft drinks, cereals, athletic goods and games, credit cards, and insurance companies. And now even rental cars, too.

If you prefer Saturday morning cartoons to commercials, you'll see Wayne with fellow superstars, Bo Jackson and Michael Jordan, in *Pro-Stars* — General Mills' version of cereal-TV. Add to this his charity organizations, and Wayne's clients are as numerous as ex-Oilers in Los Angeles.

Though we still miss him and love him, do we buy all he's pushing besides pucks?

From the moment Wayne signed on centre ice, the night of his 18th birthday, it was obvious endorsement opportunities would soon follow him right into the locker room.

He mounted credibility with the advertisers as easily as he stacked up scoring titles. By 1990, it is estimated he was earning more than $2 million per year from his endorsements.

Want to trust him

"Wayne has transcended his game like no other player," explains Michael Barnett, Wayne's business manager, speaking by phone from Los Angeles. "He's an ambassador for the sport and a role model for children."

Young NHL hopefuls carefully note the aluminum hockey stick he uses and the cereal he eats. We want to trust him.

Why is it, then, about 30 per cent of consumers don't believe celebrity endorsers actually use the products they promote, and 50 per cent of us believe they do it only for the money? This according to a survey by one New York advertising/research company.

It may be because celebrity athletes like Wayne need to appeal to us with more than mere superstar status.

Not only should they be experts on the field, on the court, or on the ice, they should also have an affinity to the product beyond just being able to stress the syllables of the brand name correctly.

Experts from one advertising research company, Gallup & Robinson of New Jersey, have concluded celebrity appropriateness is the single most important determinant in both attracting attention and persuasiveness.

So the fact that Bo Jackson wears his Nikes both on-camera and off, Jackie Stewart consults with Ford engineers to improve the handling of new cars, or Larvin "Magic" Johnson has the courage to speak on behalf of AIDS, may not only stop us flipping channels for a few seconds, but may also change the way we think about a product or even a terrifying disease.

When it comes to endorsements for hockey equipment — first Titan-Jofa, now Easton — Wayne's expertise shines.

But he has also smiled for Canon Cameras,

Lloyd's Bank of Canada and recently began promoting car rentals for Thrifty, who offer customers a copy of Wayne's book Gretzky in return for a donation to The Braille Literacy Foundation.

Yet no matter how much a wealthy athlete needs a bank, unless we're used to that person in a business role, it's questionable whether he or she can speak credibly about something as weighty as financial services.

And although O.J. Simpson's mad dashes through airline terminals were a memorable gimmick for Hertz, how many professional athletes of Wayne's stature worry about whether to get the economy model or splurge on air conditioning?

One American ad executive once said: "If you can use any one of 20 celebrities in your campaign, then it's not a good idea to take the star route."

So despite remarks by the vice-president of marketing for the now defunct Lloyd's Bank, that he chose Wayne because "Wayne's the best in the world at what he does," this may be too simplistic a standard on which to build our faith in a product or the celebrity endorser.

Even if an advertiser wants a celebrity for attention-getting purposes, this is effective in just 40 per cent of commercials, according to communications researchers McCollum Spielman, of New York. Actually getting attitudes to change works in only about half the ads after that, they say.

No consumer expert has to tell us how annoying celebrity overexposure is either. Few celebrities defy the old rule that too many product categories weaken their appeal.

Celebrity impact actually softens with each ad campaign, like the glare of one more loud plaid in Don Cherry's closet. The ads all blend together.

Even Bill Cosby, with "reels" (industry jargon for portfolio) for Del Monte, Texas Instruments, Jell-O and more, took a blow to his credibility when he switched from Original to new-formula Coke.

For celebrities with less athletic personas than Cosby, strong relationships with a select group of advertisers may be just as rewarding.

Despite Bo Jackson having suffered a serious hip injury last year, Pepsi, Nike, and Cramer sports medicine products — the three companies with which Bo does business — insisted on continuing their relationships with him. Nike executives attribute annual sales increases of 25 per cent to the use of sports celebrities, in particular, to the strong identity Bo has with their company.

Deals, deals, deals

Wayne, however, has on-going deals with Coca Cola, American Express, Nike, Zurich Insurance, General Mills, Easton, Ultra Wheels, and Thrifty Rental Cars. He now decks between Diet Coke and Coke Classic, after a stint with 7-Up early on in his career.

With his diverse roster of clients, could it be that Wayne is beginning to daunt all but his strongest supporters among us?

There is the 'helluva great guy' principle, which may override unlikely brand match-ups and too much exposure.

"If we like an athlete's personality, says Sharon Heatly, Associate Professor of Marketing, University of Alabama, "we'll let him or her get away with a lot more than we would if that person were a John McEnroe."

And because we imagine our heroes to possess qualities beyond mere physical brilliance, we are often willing to grant them superstar status in everything they do. We trust their opinion about almost anything.

And maybe that's where we're at with Wayne. Edmontonians helped put him where he is. If we didn't want him on TV, advertisers would seek out someone more popular.

Given that we're living here in the Wayne belt, perhaps we have a high tolerance level for the business activities he pursues. Credibility and respect are not easily thwarted by less-than-logical relationships.

And in a city slightly short of heroes these days, where the guy who drives the Zamboni is one of the few veterans on the ice, why would we miss an opportunity to, say, reach out and touch our No. 99?

FIGURE 16

"Wayne's World."

Winning a Grey Cup was fun for Wayne and McNall, but it could never be a substitute for their unfulfilled dream of sharing a Stanley Cup win. As their various joint businesses and investments prospered, Wayne felt more pressure than ever before to reward his friend by helping to bring the Los Angeles Kings their first Stanley Cup. The dream had not been realized in three seasons with the Kings to date; perhaps it would come true during the 1991–92 season, the 75th anniversary of the NHL.

The 1991–92 Season

Wayne and Jari Kurri, reunited in Los Angeles, were expected to reenact their glorious point-scoring days in Edmonton, but fate decreed otherwise. For one thing, it didn't help the Kings's cause that Jari Kurri had the least productive season of his NHL career, finishing with 23 goals and 60 points. For another thing, Wayne was hurting at the beginning of the season. No sooner had he returned home injured from the Canada Cup tournament in September than it was time for the preseason NHL exhibition games, and so, as Rick Reilly wrote in *Sports Illustrated*, Wayne "rushed his poor lumbar into action to help his boss fill the outdoor arena at Caesar's Palace in Las Vegas for an exhibition game against the New York Rangers." During the game, he received a check in the wrong part of his back, and as a result started the regular season in the poorest shape ever, a fact that was reflected in his play. By mid-October, Wayne had played in five straight games without scoring a goal and was feeling somewhat disheartened by his lack of contribution. On 16 October, he was taking a pregame midday rest at his new home just outside Beverly Hills, when he received an urgent telephone call from his sister in Ontario. What Kim told Wayne suddenly made his problems insignificant: his father had suffered a brain aneurysm.

Anyone who has ever seen Wayne and his father together or read what they have to say about each other cannot help but be aware of the special bond between them. In Wayne's epilogue to his father's book, he writes, "Some day if I'm lucky, maybe

I'll take my son out on the ice at the farm, or play with him on the rink in the back yard in Brantford. And when he comes in, crying a little because his feet are frozen, I'll hold his toes and make the cold go away, just like my Dad did for me."

Kim Gretzky was calling from the farm, where she had lived since their grandmother died, and where their father had been stricken. Walter Gretzky had retired from Bell Telephone in May 1991, at the age of 52, having qualified for his full pension. A man of old-fashioned values and simple tastes, he had always resisted his son's attempts to reward him with a more lavish home or a luxury car, and preferred to keep busy in his own way. He was painting his late mother's old farmhouse when the aneurysm occurred, and he was rushed to Hamilton General Hospital.

On hearing the news, Wayne informed McNall, and he was immediately released from Kings duty. He chartered a plane and, with Janet, their two children, and his brother Keith, who was staying with them, flew to his father's side. "Our thoughts and prayers are with Wayne and his family," said McNall, a sentiment shared by teammates, friends, and hockey fans everywhere. Wayne's mother, sister, and other brothers joined him in the intensive-care unit, to hear a doctor's warning that Walter might not survive the night.

A delicate operation three days later by neurosurgeon Rocco de Villiers took Walter Gretzky past the life-or-death situation. Two months earlier, de Villiers' 19-year-old daughter had been kidnapped, raped, and murdered in Burlington, Ontario, and people around the hospital were of the opinion that saving Walter Gretzky had been therapeutic for him in a sense. "It's kind of like God's way of rekindling a fire in this guy," said Wayne, relieved as his father's condition improved. After the operation, in fact, Walter Gretzky was able to speak coherently to his family. His condition gradually improved; by 28 October, Wayne was able to return to the Kings, by November his father was joking with him about his play, and by December Walter was able to spend Christmas at home with his family.

Slump and Recovery

Wayne returned to the Kings's lineup after missing five games, and recorded an assist on Jari Kurri's third-period goal, but he failed to score his first goal of the season. Wayne's return gave his team a boost, and the Kings defeated the Red Wings 4–3 in Detroit. Afterwards, Wayne said, "This is just a game, my family comes first. Playing hockey doesn't get my dad out of my mind. It couldn't." But he was a professional hockey player, under contract, with an unfulfilled team ambition, and he was expected to perform, by his father as much as by anyone else.

So he was back on the ice, but his performance was dismal by any standard, let alone what was expected of the Great One. Wayne was in the worst slump of his career; he was so depressed that he told Janet, "This is the end. . . . I never, ever dreamed I could play this bad," and seriously contemplated retirement from the game he loved — at the age of 30. To the Kings's assistant coach, Cap Raeder, he said, "I hate mediocrity. If there's one thing I can't accept, it's mediocrity." His productivity was way down, and his team was suffering. In one 0–4–2 stretch for the Kings in early November, Wayne contributed just three points. By 19 November, he had been held pointless in four of his last six games, scoring only one goal during that span. His wife and friends talked him out of retirement, however, and Raeder told him to relax and have fun. Meanwhile, his father's condition slowly improved. Then suddenly it all turned around. As Rick Reilly put it, in an article in *Sports Illustrated*, "Gretzky went ballistic — six goals and 15 assists in nine games, including a hat trick." Once again, Wayne would be a factor in the NHL individual scoring race, and, to top it off, his horse Golden Pheasant won the $2.77 million Japan Cup. Life was good again, on and off the ice, thoughts of retirement receded, and, early in the new year, a trade provided some fresh momentum to the Kings's Stanley Cup ambitions.

On 19 February 1992, the Kings obtained Wayne's close friend, Paul Coffey, from the Pittsburgh Penguins. Acknowledged as one of the best skaters ever in the NHL, Coffey was expected to eclipse the scoring marks for defencemen in the league, and to improve the Kings's prospects significantly. He was yet another one of those ex-Edmonton Oilers with considerable Stanley Cup-winning experience, including one with the Penguins at the end of the previous season. Although the Kings had traded Mike Krushelnyski to Toronto in November of 1990, they now had no fewer than five ex-Oilers on the roster: Gretzky, Coffey, Huddy, Kurri, and McSorley. This fact was not lost on the media, and McNall was seen to be trying to purchase a Stanley Cup by importing proven Oiler talent. In February 1993, *Hockey Illustrated* asked, "Can the Great One and the rest of the aging Oiler Alumni Association rebound this year?" while the *Inside Hockey Yearbook '93* commented, "Edmonton South has shown it isn't as good as Edmonton North was or is, and compounding the problem is a lack of good, young prospects." However, if the acquisition of Paul Coffey led to a first Stanley Cup, the Kings would be happy to live with any criticism.

What no one envisaged at the time of the Coffey trade was that, for the first time in NHL history, there might not actually be any Stanley Cup play-offs in the spring of 1992. In fact, when the Kings played the Oilers on 29 March at Northlands Coliseum, in a 2–2 tie, it looked like it might be the last game of the season. Three days later, the NHL Players's Association (NHLPA) was on strike, and Wayne was in a difficult position.

A Diplomatic Role

The NHL's 75th anniversary season, 1991–92, was supposed to be a celebration of hockey history, but it was threatened with disruption from the start. In June of 1991, talks between owners and the NHLPA made little progress: the owners were claiming that soaring salaries could kill the league, and the players were calling for total free agency and no entry draft. The collective agreement had expired on 15 September, and the owners presented revised proposals to the players for consideration. On 1 January 1992, Bob Goodenow, the NHLPA's deputy director, replaced Alan Eagleson as executive director; the deadlocked talks dragged on. The owners made their "final offer" on 28 March, and the players's counterproposal was rejected the next day. The NHLPA then delayed an original 30 March deadline for further consultations, but finally announced the first-ever players's strike on 2 April.

League president John Zeigler, representing the owners, and Goodenow both realized that neither side's position would find total favour with the public. In difficult economic times, the owners were seen to be making too much profit and the players were perceived as greedy and overpaid. What sympathy existed for either side's point of view was tempered by the fact that any settlement reached would likely result in higher ticket prices to pay for it. But the fans' anger and resentment was fuelled most of all by the cruel timing of their deprivation, at the culmination of the regular season, when the play-offs determine the Stanley Cup champion and NHL hockey is always at its most exciting. Canadians would feel the loss most. Hockey was their game, and Canada would be a miserable place without this annual rite of spring. As the 13 April 1992 issue of *Maclean's* said, "For fans, the play-offs are eight weeks of sudden-death hockey, the steaming-hot main course after a regular season of lukewarm appetizers. For the players, the play-offs are their greatest test, their reason for competing." In the same article, Wayne put things in a nutshell: "There'll be no sympathy for our side. There'll be no sympathy for the owners. The sport will be tarnished."

The strike put Wayne in an uncomfortable situation, presenting him with perhaps the most peculiar challenge of his career. He may have been offstage when Goodenow and Zeigler went head-to-head as official representatives of the two warring sides, but he was busy and influential behind the scenes. Described in the *Edmonton Sun* as "forever the diplomat," Wayne certainly needed to play that role during those April days, as the strike placed him and his friend Bruce McNall on opposite sides of the fence. *Maclean's* remarked, "Of the 564 members of the players's association, the one with the most to lose from a strike was Wayne Gretzky," because he commanded the league's highest salary, and because of his "close friendship and business relationship" with McNall; but it also reported that "Gretzky maintained his solidarity with his teammates."

People wondered if the strike would cost Wayne his friendship with McNall. Admitting to being torn by divided loyalties when the strike appeared imminent, Wayne said, in the 23 March 1992 edition of the *Edmonton Journal*, "The hardest part is we get so well-treated in Los Angeles. It's not right. The other side of it is you can get traded to another team and all of a sudden, you don't have the same owner." There were several issues to be resolved, but hockey-card licensing, free agency, and the length of contracts were the most serious. However, even while both sides waited for the other to blink, both had too much to lose not to come to a sensible arrangement quickly. So despite deadlines, insults, take-or-leave-it edicts, and doomsday scenarios, a settlement was reached on 19 April.

Wayne was looked to by the players for guidance, beyond the leadership provided by the NHLPA representatives. Ed Johnston, general manager of the Hartford Whalers, was quoted as saying, "When Wayne Gretzky talks, everybody listens." Although the precise details of Wayne's conversations are unknown, he obviously did a lot of talking, and the players listened. According to owner Peter Pocklington, Wayne played a significant part in the 48 hours before settlement was reached, by making up to 100 telephone calls. "Wayne talked to everybody," said Mark Messier, another of several high-profile players involved. In the end, Wayne's fourth season with the Kings turned out to be one of the least satisfactory and successful in his experience. He recorded 31 goals and 121 points, the lowest totals of his NHL career — still good enough for third place in the league, but hardly up to the usual Gretzky standard. Not only that, but for the first time in his NHL career Wayne was not selected for either the first or the second all-star team, and the only NHL trophy he won in 1992 was his third Lady Byng Trophy (for sportsmanship). The Los Angeles Kings finished tied with the Boston Bruins for ninth place in the league, scoring 53 fewer goals than they had the previous season, and were again eliminated in the first round of the play-offs by the Edmonton Oilers, in six games. Although Wayne alone could not be blamed — and could point to valid extenuating circumstances — the personal disappointment that he felt in April of 1992 was very hard to bear.

A Fateful Year

During the summer, Wayne played golf and tennis, kept in shape, and then reported to the Kings's training camp for the 1992–93 season. He left camp on 13 September to be with his wife for the birth of their third child, Trevor Douglas — and then he had to check into hospital himself only two days later.

Wayne was experiencing pain in the chest area, but he was admitted for treatment of what was called back strain. He underwent traction for two days, and then rested, before being released from hospital on 22 September. At a press conference that day, Dr. Robert Watkins said that tests had determined that Wayne was suffering from a herniated thoracic disc, which was putting intense pressure on a nerve between the ribs. Although the prognosis, given proper treatment and rehabilitation, was optimistic, it was a serious, potentially career-ending injury. Wayne said he had experienced chest and rib pain in "March, April and May" of the previous season, and believed that his back injury stemmed from hits from behind that he had sustained over the years. As only one of several players hampered by back injuries in recent years, including Mike Bossy, Wendell Clark, and Mario Lemieux, he expressed concern that as players were getting bigger, faster, and stronger, the NHL must crack down on players who check from behind, a proposal enthusiastically endorsed by Bruce McNall and other concerned hockey fans. Two months later, it was reported that Wayne was expected to be back in the Los Angeles Kings's lineup in March of 1993.

Actually, Wayne missed only 39 games while recuperating and surprised everyone by returning to the Kings's lineup on 6 January 1993, in a game against the Tampa Bay Lightning. It was his 1,000th NHL game, but the celebration was muted because the Kings lost. Around Christmastime the team had been doing very well under new coach Barry Melrose, and were battling for first place in the Smythe Division. Then, a free-fall began as the Kings experienced a winless streak. Not surprisingly, Wayne's form was somewhat erratic after his layoff, which didn't help the Kings's fortunes. On 8 January he scored his first two goals of the season against the Winnipeg Jets (although the Kings lost 6–3), but didn't score again until 17 February when the Kings routed the Minnesota North Stars 10–5. This was — for Wayne — an unprecedented goalless drought of 16 games. The Kings then mounted a late-season surge, and finished third in the Smythe Division. Wayne himself, playing in only 45 games, finished the 1992–93 season with a more than respectable total of 16 goals and 49 assists for 65 points. It was an optimistic group of players that went into the playoffs: the Los Angeles Kings had never before progressed beyond the Smythe Division Final, but this year would be different.

The Kings's First Stanley Cup Final

The Kings's confidence was justified: they disposed of the second-place Calgary Flames in the first round and the division-winning Vancouver Canucks in the next round, to put themselves in the Campbell Conference final against the Toronto Maple Leafs. The Leafs were making their first appearance in a Stanley Cup semifinal since 1978 (they last won the Cup in 1967), after getting past the Detroit Red Wings and St. Louis Blues in two stirring seven-game series. Increasing the anticipation was the fact that Wayne, the kid from nearby Brantford who grew up to be the Great One, would be making his first NHL play-off appearance in Toronto.

What transpired was another dramatic seven-game series in which the Kings eventually prevailed. With the series tied at three games apiece, and the seventh game being held at Maple Leaf Gardens, many fans had visions of an all-Canadian Montreal Canadiens–Toronto Maple Leafs Stanley Cup final, an event that last happened twenty-six years earlier, when it had been the highlight of the nation's centennial year celebrations. Their hope was fuelled by the outstanding form of Leafs's players such as (ex-Oiler) Glenn Anderson, captain Wendell Clark, Doug Gilmour, and goalie Felix Potvin, and by the fact that Wayne was having, for him, a rather indifferent play-off series.

Rumours circulated about his "back problem," and he had suffered a cracked rib in a game against the Calgary Flames in the first round, and had surgery to repair an ingrowing toenail just before the series against the Leafs. Indeed, a headline in a Toronto newspaper after game five said Wayne Gretzky looked like he was playing with a piano on his back — just the sort of comment that was bound to spur him to make another larger-than-life achievement. Wayne scored the winning goal in the next two games; in game seven, which the Kings won 5-4, he actually scored three goals and added an assist, to help propel his team into its first Stanley Cup final. The elated Kings's coach Barry Melrose was later quoted in the *Edmonton Sun*: "People who say that he wasn't — or isn't — the greatest player in hockey, are nuts."

Now the NHL had a final series that would keep hockey fans on both sides of the border glued to their TV sets. As an editorial in the *Edmonton Sun* put it:

On one side you have the Los Angeles Kings — a mega-media centre and home of Wayne Gretzky, the greatest, most popular and most respected player the game has ever known.

On the other side you have the Montreal Canadiens, the most storied and decorated team in all of hockey. Perhaps in all of sports.

The Kings were going for their first Stanley Cup, the Canadiens vying for their unparalleled 24th, and everything promised that this would be a great season finale. It was noted, too, that Wayne had won his first Stanley Cup in his fifth season with the Edmonton Oilers, and this was now his fifth season with the Kings. Perhaps it was an omen, a sign that his ambition to win the trophy for his employer — and friend — Bruce McNall, was about to be realized.

It certainly looked promising after the first game, despite an early mistake by Wayne, who accidentally tipped the puck past his own goalkeeper, thus allowing the Canadiens to tie the score at 1-1. The Kings then went on to win by four goals to one, and Wayne atoned for his uncharacteristic error with another outstanding individual display. He picked up four points, causing Canadiens's coach Jacques Demers to admit afterwards that "Gretzky toyed with us tonight." In the second game, the Kings were leading 2–1 until the discovery that Marty McSorley was using an illegal stick resulted in his being sent to the penalty box, thus allowing Eric Desjardins of the Canadiens to tie the game with only one minute and 13 seconds remaining. Then, Desjardins scored again, at 51 seconds into overtime, making this the first ever three-goal game by a defenceman in a Stanley Cup final. In game three in Los Angeles, the Kings fought back from a 3–0 deficit to level terms, only to see the Canadiens's John LeClair score another overtime winner, this time after only 34 seconds. Incredibly, LeClair also scored the overtime winner in game four (in these 1993 play-offs, the Canadiens would win no less than 10 games in overtime) for a 3–2 victory and a commanding 3–1 lead in games to take back to Montreal for game five.

The Canadiens's tenacity proved too much for the Kings, and the Montreal team went on to win their 24th Stanley Cup after a 4–1 victory in the fifth game. It was a heartbreaking loss for the Kings, but reaching the Stanley Cup final for the first time was a great accomplishment. Wayne himself finished as the play-off's individual scoring leader, with 15 goals and 40 points. At the end of game five, Wayne gave the Montreal coach his hockey stick, which Demers had requested as a birthday present for his son.

Predictably, rumours soon began to circulate about Wayne's possible retirement. The rumours only increased with the news that, for the first time since he had entered the league, Wayne was not a finalist for any NHL award. Wayne has refused to provide the media with a definite answer to their many questions, saying he needs more time to make the decision about his future.

Wayne's Life So Far

Since Wayne is only 32 years old, any Gretzky biography can only really be an account of an unfinished life, spent almost entirely in the world of hockey. It is quite possible that his athletic career will continue for some time, unless his recent serious injuries cause him to retire prematurely from the game he loves. Even if he retires in the near future, he has more than earned his title "the Great One." But if he continues? Apart from the unfulfilled quest to bring a Stanley Cup to Los Angeles, Wayne has also expressed a desire to play in the Olympics, but it now appears unlikely that NHL players will be allowed to compete in the 1994 Winter Olympic Games. Another possibility would be to own an NHL franchise, though Wayne believes that the cost would probably be prohibitive; however, he does not want to coach or be a general manager. He mentions in his autobiography that he'd like to bring a National Basketball Association franchise to Toronto one day. He also writes about records (including his own) being made to be broken, and at present he is only 37 goals shy of breaking Gordie Howe's record of 801 goals in NHL regular seasons. Anyone who has followed the Wayne Gretzky story knows that nothing is impossible.

To his legions of admirers, Wayne's statistics speak for themselves. He owns or shares no less than 58 NHL records, and has won all the individual awards for which he is eligible, several times over, more than any other player; many of his records will probably never be equalled.

Yet for all his irrefutable claims to greatness, Wayne Gretzky has never won the hearts of all hockey fans. He will always lack the rugged, "macho" element that many fans look for in their traditional hockey heroes, epitomized by "Mr. Hockey," Gordie Howe. Howe had another nickname: "Mr. Elbows"; he never needed a bodyguard, and he was no stranger to the penalty box. Howe's brief profile in *The Canadian Encyclopedia* ends, "Howe dominated his sport as much by his intimidating strength as by his mastery of skills; he also accumulated 2419 minutes in penalties." Howe personified the Conn Smythe dictum "If you can't lick 'em in the alley, you can't beat 'em on the ice." Gretzky, for all his skill, never had Howe's "intimidating strength."

In the glory years of the 1980s, Wayne led the Edmonton Oilers to four of their five Stanley Cups, before he was traded to the L.A. Kings. During this time, more than any other single player, Wayne Gretzky exposed the crude limitations of Smythe's words, demonstrating that — within the rules — there is simply no substitute for pure individual skill allied with team speed. His consistent personal campaign against fighting and violence would never endear him to the devotees of "rock 'em, sock 'em hockey"; in fact, one of Wayne's shortcomings, according to hockey pundit Don Cherry, is that "he has become the social conscience of hockey."

Of course, every sport adapts and changes over time in order to survive, and in this periodic process of self-examination a conscience of sorts is essential. Wayne Gretzky's contribution to hockey in this respect has been well summed up by American sports historian Richard Crepeau:

Every decade or so an athlete comes along who takes his or her sport to new and higher levels. The standards of excellence are raised. The artistry of play is elaborated. Things are done which have never been done before. Long-standing records are broken. The fans flock to see the new star become the hero. It's all remarkable and very exciting, worthy of great plaudits. But only once in a lifetime does an athlete appear who totally redefines a sport. This is what Wayne Gretzky has done. This is why in 50 or 100 years the name Gretzky will stand alone when the athletes of the second half of the 20th Century are discussed.

Chronology

1930s   European immigrants Tony and Mary Gretzky leave the United States and buy 25 acres of farmland in Canning, Ontario. They have six children, including Walter Gretzky.

1961   Wayne Douglas Gretzky, the first child of Walter and Phyllis Gretzky, is born on 26 January in Brantford, where Walter works for the Bell Telephone Company. Other children include Kim (born in 1963), Keith (1966), Glen (1968), and Brent (1972).

1963   Wayne has his first skate on the Nith River at his grandparents' farm.

1967–68   Six-year-old Wayne (playing with 10-year-olds), scores his first (and only) goal of the season for the Novice A Division Nadrofsky Steelers of the Brantford Atom League.

1968–69   Wayne scores 27 goals for the Nadrofsky Steelers.

1969–70   Wayne scores 104 goals for the Nadrofsky Steelers, plus 63 assists, in 62 games.

1970–71   Wayne scores 196 goals for the Nadrofsky Steelers, plus 120 assists, in 76 games.

1971–72   Wayne scores an incredible 378 goals during his final year as a novice. His feats attract national media attention. He is called "the Great Gretzky," "the next Bobby Orr," and so on.

1972   Eleven-year-old Wayne is featured in the April issue of *Canadian Magazine*; he sits at the head table at the Kiwanis "Great Men of Sport" dinner with his idol, Gordie Howe.

1972–73   Wayne scores 105 goals in major peewee league play, playing for Turkstra Lumber.

1973–74 Wayne scores 192 goals for Turkstra Lumber, including goal number 1,000, on 10 April 1974.

1974–75 In his final minor hockey season, Wayne scores 90 goals, playing for the Charcon Chargers.

1975 Fourteen-year-old Wayne moves to Toronto, lives with the Cormishes, enrols in West Humber Collegiate Institute (Summer).

1975–76 Wayne plays Junior B Hockey (with 20-year-olds) for the Vaughan Nationals of the Metropolitan Toronto Hockey League, finishes the season with 27 goals and 33 assists, and wins the league's Rookie-of-the-Year award.

1976–77 Wayne plays his second year of Junior B hockey with the Seneca Nationals of the MTHL, scoring 36 goals and 26 assists.

1977 Wayne stars as the youngest player on the national junior team in the world junior tournament at Montreal, in December, by leading all scorers, and is the only Canadian selected for the all-star team.

1977–78 Wayne moves to Sault Ste. Marie, lives with the Bodnars, sets records for the Soo Greyhounds of the OHA, wins several awards, and adopts sweater number 99. His exploits attract the attention of professional scouts from both the National Hockey League and the World Hockey Association.

1978 Wayne becomes a professional hockey player at age 17, when Nelson Skalbania signs him to a four-year contract (worth almost $1 million) with the Indianapolis Racers of the WHA. Wayne plays only eight games with the Racers before being traded to the Edmonton Oilers.

1979 On his 18th birthday (26 January), Wayne is signed to a 21-year contract "until 1999" by owner Peter Pocklington, who pays him approximately $300,000 per year. Wayne begins a steady relationship with Edmonton-born singer Vikki Moss, his constant companion for the next eight years.

1979–80   The WHA merges with the NHL. Wayne finishes his first NHL season with 137 points, tied for the league scoring title. He wins the first of nine Hart Memorial Trophies (eight of them consecutively from 1980 to 1987; the other in 1989); his first Lady Byng Trophy, the sportsmanship award (won again in 1991 and 1992); and plays in the NHL all-star game, the first of 13 such appearances (1980–86; 1988–93).

1980–81   Wayne finishes his second NHL season with 164 points (55 goals and 109 assists), setting records. He breaks Phil Esposito's single-season points record of 152 (30 March 1981) and Bobby Orr's single-season assist record of 102 (1 April 1981), and becomes the first player in NHL history to average more than two points per game. Wayne wins the first of nine Art Ross Trophies, the league scoring title (seven of them consecutive from 1981 to 1987, the others in 1990 and 1991).

1981   The first annual Wayne Gretzky Celebrity Tennis Tournament is held in Brantford (June); over the next decade it raises more than $1 million for the Canadian National Institute for the Blind. Wayne plays in his first Canada Cup tournament (September); he finishes as individual scoring leader with 12 points, but Canada loses in the final to the USSR. Wayne first meets 16-year-old Janet Jones, his future bride; their paths cross several times through mutual acquaintances, but there is no "spark" until 1987. Wayne makes a forgettable acting début on the television soap opera *The Young and the Restless*. Wayne is named Athlete of the Year by the *Sporting News*. Mike Barnett becomes Wayne's marketing manager in Edmonton. Wayne becomes the first player in the NHL to score 50 goals in fewer than 50 games, by scoring five goals against the Philadelphia Flyers, in only his 39th game of the season (30 December).

1981–82   Wayne finishes the season with 92 goals, 120 assists, 212 points, and 10 hat-tricks, all NHL records.

1982   Wayne turns 21 (26 January), and Pocklington gives

him a new contract worth approximately $1 million per year, plus property in western Canada. Wayne is the NHL's plus/minus leader for first time, winning the Emory Edge Award (which he wins again in 1983, 1984, 1985, and 1987). He also wins the Lester B. Pearson Award, as the players's selection for the NHL's outstanding player (he wins it again in 1983, 1984, 1985, and 1987), and is named Sportsman of the Year by *Sports Illustrated*. Wayne, family, and friends visit the USSR to shoot a television special with famous Russian goalkeeper Vladislav Tretiak (July). Wayne wins the Lou Marsh Award as Canada's outstanding male athlete (which he wins again in 1983, 1985, and 1989).

1982–83   Wayne finishes the season with 196 points (71 goals and 125 assists); he plays in his first Stanley Cup final, but the Edmonton Oilers are beaten in four straight games by the New York Islanders.

1983–84   In his first season as captain of the Oilers, Wayne finishes with 87 goals, 118 assists, and 205 points. He sets NHL records for most shorthanded goals in a season (12); longest consecutive assist-scoring streak (17); and longest consecutive point-scoring streak (51).

1984   Wayne leads the Oilers to their first Stanley Cup, winning over the New York Islanders; in 19 play-off games, he scores 13 goals and 22 assists. Wayne plays in his second Canada Cup; Canada defeats Sweden in the final; Wayne again leads individual scoring, with 12 points. Walter's book about his son, *Gretzky* (coauthored by Jim Taylor), is published.

1984–85   Wayne completes his third 200-plus-points season and leads the Oilers to a second Stanley Cup, winning over the Philadelphia Flyers. He wins his first Conn Smythe Trophy as the play-offs MVP (most valuable player) and the first of three consecutive Chrysler-Dodge NHL Performer of the Year Awards. Wayne's fear of flying is at its worst around this time; he tries several remedies, and the problem recedes.

1985–86   Wayne completes the season with a record 215 points, the highest in NHL history, but the Oilers lose to the Calgary Flames in the play-offs.

1986–87   Wayne completes the season as leader in goals (62), assists (121), and points (183), for the fifth time in eight years; scores his 500th goal (22 November 1986); and leads the Oilers to a third Stanley Cup with a victory over the Philadelphia Flyers.

1987   Wayne's long relationship with Vikki Moss, under strain for some time, ends after she moves to Los Angeles to pursue her career. Wayne meets Janet Jones again, and this time they fall in love. Janet accompanies him to the Canada Cup tournament in August/September, where their friendship becomes public knowledge. Wayne plays in his third Canada Cup tournament. Canada defeats the USSR in the three-game final, and Wayne again leads individual scoring with 21 points. *The Boys on the Bus*, a video documentary about the Edmonton Oilers during the 1986–87 season, is released.

1987–88   Wayne misses 16 games due to injury. He still leads the NHL in assists (109), but has his first season with fewer than 50 goals (40). He leads Oilers to a fourth Stanley Cup, winning over the Boston Bruins. He sets a play-offs record of 43 points and wins his second Conn Smythe Trophy.

1988   Wayne proposes to Janet by telephone and is accepted (10 January). Their engagement is announced and the wedding date is set for July. Wayne and Janet are married at St. Joseph's Basilica in Edmonton (16 July). Wayne is traded to Los Angeles Kings in what is described as biggest trade in sports history (9 August). In his first game with L.A. Kings, a home opener against the Detroit Red Wings before a sellout crowd, Wayne scores with his first shot, and gets three assists, as Kings win 8–2 (16 October). Wayne plays his first game in the Kings uniform at Northlands Coliseum, Edmonton. The sellout crowd gives him a great ovation, but the Kings lose 8–6 (19 October).

Wayne scores his 600th NHL goal in Detroit. (23 November). Paulina Mary Jean Gretzky is born (19 December).

1988–89　Wayne finishes his first season with L.A. Kings with 54 goals and 114 points. The Kings move up from 18th place to 4th in the NHL, and are 2nd in the Smythe Division. They defeat the Edmonton Oilers in the first round of the play-offs, but lose to the Calgary Flames in the division final.

1989　A life-sized statue of Wayne is erected outside Northlands Coliseum, Edmonton (27 August). Wayne breaks Gordie Howe's all-time points record (1,850) in the NHL (15 October).

1989–90　Wayne finishes his second season with the L.A. Kings with 40 goals and 102 assists (missing seven games due to injury). The Kings lose the Smythe divisional final to the Oilers in four straight games, and Wayne is injured in Game Three.

1990　Wayne is selected as Athlete of the Decade (the 1980s) in a poll conducted by Associated Press. Wayne's autobiography and two biographies are published. A biographical video entitled *Above and Beyond* is released. The Aquatic Centre in Brantford is expanded and renamed the Wayne Gretzky Sports Centre. The complex provides facilities for several sports, includes a Sports Hall of Recognition, and publishes monthly a "Gretzky Chronicle" newsletter. Wayne and Janet's second child, Ty Robert, is born (9 July). Wayne becomes the first NHL player to score 2,000 points (23 October).

1990–91　Wayne finishes his third season with the L.A. Kings with 41 goals and 122 assists, to win his ninth Art Ross trophy. The Kings finish first in the Smythe Division, third in the league, but lose to Edmonton Oilers in the divisional final.

1991　Wayne scores his 700th NHL goal (3 January). Wayne becomes part-owner of the Toronto Argonauts of the Canadian Football League, with Bruce McNall and

John Candy (March). Wayne and McNall invest around $500,000 in a rare 1910 Honus Wagner baseball card. Wayne plays in his fourth Canada Cup tournament, and again finishes as individual scoring leader (August/September). Canada wins the tournament, but Wayne misses the final game against the United States because of a serious back injury. Walter Gretzky suffers a brain aneurysm and is taken to Hamilton General Hospital (October). Wayne and other family members rush to his bedside.

1991–92   Wayne finishes the season with 31 goals and 121 points, the lowest totals of his NHL career, but wins his second Lady Byng Trophy. The Kings lose to the Oilers in the first round of the play-offs.

1992   The NHL's 75th-anniversary season is tarnished by the first NHL Players's Association strike, which threatens the play-offs. The strike lasts 10 days (2 April–12 April); Wayne is credited with playing a key role behind the scenes in obtaining a settlement. Janet and Wayne's third child, Trevor Douglas, is born (14 September). At a press conference on 22 September it is announced that Wayne is suffering from a herniated disc, a serious, potentially career-ending back injury. His return to hockey is predicted for March 1993. As of December 1992, Wayne holds or shares 58 National Hockey League records.

1993   Against all odds, Wayne returns from his injury to play his first game of the 1992–93 season (6 January). It is his 1,000th NHL game. Wayne finishes the 1992–93 season with 16 goals and 49 assists in only 45 games. In their first Stanley Cup Final, the Kings are beaten by the Montreal Canadiens in five games (three of them going to overtime). Wayne finishes as individual scoring leader in the play-offs with 15 goals and 25 assists. Before, during, and after the play-offs, trade or retirement rumours concerning Wayne's future circulate.

APPENDIX

Career Totals, 1976-1993

SEASON	CLUB	LEAGUE	GP	G	A	PTS	GP	G	A	PTS
1976–77	Peterborough	OHA	3	0	3	3	-	-	-	-
1977–78	Sault Ste. Marie	OHA	64	70	112	182	13	6	20	26
1978–79	Indianapolis	WHA	8	3	3	6	-	-	-	-
	Edmonton	WHA	72	43	61	104	13	10	10	20
1979–80	Edmonton	NHL	79	51	86	137	3	2	1	3
1980–81	Edmonton	NHL	80	55	109	164	9	7	14	21
1981–82	Edmonton	NHL	80	92	120	212	5	5	7	12
1982–83	Edmonton	NHL	80	71	125	196	16	12	26	38
1983–84	Edmonton	NHL	74	87	118	205	19	13	22	35
1984–85	Edmonton	NHL	80	73	135	208	18	17	30	47
1985–86	Edmonton	NHL	80	52	163	215	10	8	11	19
1986–87	Edmonton	NHL	79	62	121	183	21	5	29	34
1987–88	Edmonton	NHL	64	40	109	149	19	12	31	43
1988–89	Los Angeles	NHL	78	54	114	168	11	5	17	22
1989–90	Los Angeles	NHL	73	40	102	142	7	3	7	10
1990–91	Los Angeles	NHL	78	41	122	163	12	4	11	15
1991–92	Los Angeles	NHL	74	31	90	121	6	2	5	7
1992–93	Los Angeles	NHL	45	16	49	65	24	15	25	40
NHL Totals			1044	765	1563	2328	180	110	236	346
WHA Totals			80	46	64	110	13	10	10	20
Professional Totals			1124	811	1627	2438	193	120	246	366

WORKS CONSULTED

Barnes, Dan. "The End." *Edmonton Sun* 8 Apr. 1992: 51.

Benagh, Jim. *Picture Story of Wayne Gretzky*. New York: Messner, 1982.

The Boys on the Bus. Videocassette. Dir. Bob McKeown. A McKeown/ McGee Film. Produced in conjunction with Hawkherst Enterprises and The Molson Breweries of Canada, 1987.

Burchard, S.H. *Sports Star: Wayne Gretzky*. New York: Harcourt, 1982.

Came, Barry. "Passion's Prize." *Maclean's* 21 June 1993: 58–59.

Carpenter, Susan, et al. *The Los Angeles Kings 1991–92 Media Guide*. N.p.: Steele, [1992].

Coffey, Phil. "Wayne Gretzky: The King." *Hockey Illustrated* Apr. 1991: 6–11.

——. "The Great One: Thirtysomething and Going Strong." *Hockey Illustrated* Feb. 1992: 38–42.

Cole, Cam. "99 Cheers." *Edmonton Journal* 2 June 1993: D1.

Crepeau, Richard C. "Gretzky's Artistry Redefines Sports." *Orlando Sentinel* 20 Jan. 1991: C13.

Cruise, David, and Alison Griffiths. *Net Worth: Exploding the Myths of Pro Hockey*. Toronto: Penguin, 1992.

Dalgish, Brenda. "Antiques and Athletes." *Maclean's* 6 May 1991: 45.

Deacon, James. "A Costly Faceoff." *Maclean's* 13 Apr. 1992: 16–18.

Diamond, Dan, ed. *The Official National Hockey League 75th Anniversary Commemorative Book*. Toronto: McClelland, 1991.

Dryden, Ken. *The Game: A Reflective and Thought-Provoking Look at Life in Hockey*. Toronto: Macmillan, 1983.

Falla, Jack. "Man with a Streak of Pure Genius." *Sports Illustrated* 23 Jan. 1984: 32–36.

Fell, Adam, et al. *Los Angeles Kings 1992–93 Media Guide*. N.p.: Steele, [1993].

Fischler, Stan. *Golden Ice: The Greatest Teams in Hockey History*. New York: Wynwood, 1990.

——. "The King of Kings." *Inside Sports* Dec. 1991: 72–77.

"Go Home and Pack." *Edmonton Sun* 1 Apr. 1987: 55.

"Gretzky's Return Pumps Up Kings." *Edmonton Journal* 17 Oct. 1991: E1.

Gretzky, Walter, and Jim Taylor. *Gretzky: From the Back Yard Rink to the Stanley Cup.* Toronto: McClelland, 1984.

Gretzky, Wayne, and Rick Reilly. *Gretzky: An Autobiography.* Toronto: Harper, 1990.

Gzowski, Peter. *The Game of Our Lives.* Toronto: Macmillan, 1983.

Hanks, Stephen. *Wayne Gretzky.* New York: St. Martin's, 1990.

Haskins, Scott. "One-on-One with Gretzky." *Edmonton Sun* 10 Apr. 1987: 58.

—. "Vikki!" *Edmonton Sun* 3 Apr. 1987: 64.

Inside Hockey Yearbook '93 6.1 (1992).

Jones, Terry. "The Bruce and Wayne Show." *Edmonton Sun* 22 Apr. 1991: 38–39.

—. "Gretz Gets the Winner?" *Edmonton Sun* 10 Apr. 1992: 81.

—. *The Great Gretzky.* Don Mills, ON: General, 1980.

—. *The Great Gretzky Yearbook II: The Greatest Single Season in Hockey History.* Don Mills, ON: General, 1982.

Knowles, S., ed. *Edmonton Oilers 1991–1992 Official Guide.* N.p.: The Edmonton Oilers, [1992].

Leder, Jane Mersky. *Wayne Gretzky.* Mankato, MN: Crestwood, 1985.

Lowe, Kevin, Stan Fischler, and Shirley Fischler. *Champions: The Making of the Edmonton Oilers.* Toronto: Fawcett, 1988.

Lupicka, Mike. "Hockey's Only Hope." *Esquire* Feb. 1989: 55–57.

Marsh, James. "Gretzky, Wayne." *The Canadian Encyclopedia.* 1988 ed.

—. "Howe, Gordon." *The Canadian Encyclopedia.* 2nd ed. Edmonton: Hurtig, 1988.

—. "Stanley Cup." *The Canadian Encyclopedia.* 2nd ed. Edmonton: Hurtig, 1988.

Matheson, Jim. "Gretzky Gone." *Edmonton Journal* 10 Aug. 1988: A1.

—. "Gretzky between McNall, Players' Association." *Edmonton Journal* 23 Mar. 1992: D4.

—. "Oiler Win Cuts 99 to Heart." *Edmonton Journal* 29 Apr. 1992: D1.

McFadden, Fred. *Wayne Gretzky.* Markham, ON: Fitzhenry, 1990.

McKenzie, Jock. Personal Interview. 13 Apr. 1992.

National Hockey League Official Guide and Record Book 1992–92. N.p.: National Hockey League, 1991.

Nichols, Mark. "The 'Royal' Wedding." *Maclean's* 25 July 1988: 30–35.

Quinn, Hal. "The Glory of Gretzky." *Maclean's* 22 Feb. 1982: 36–40.

Raber, Thomas R. *Wayne Gretzky: Hockey Great.* Minneapolis: Lerner, 1991.

Reilly, Rick. "Looking to a Great Recovery." *Sports Illustrated* 16 Dec. 1991: 33–39.

Romain, Joseph, and James Duplacey. *Wayne Gretzky.* London: Bison, 1992.

Safarik, Allan, and Dolores Reimer. *Quotations from Chairman Cherry.* Vancouver: Arsenal, 1992.

———. *Quotations on the Great One: The Little Book of Wayne Gretzky.* Vancouver: Arsenal, 1992.

Scher, Jon. "King of the Kings." *Sports Illustrated* 7 June 1993: 32–33.

Semenko, Dave. *Looking Out for Number One.* Toronto: General, 1990.

Short, John. "The Toughest Part of the Game." *Edmonton Journal* 22 May 1992: F4.

"Smythe, Conn." *Colombo's Canadian Quotations.* Ed. John Robert Colombo. Edmonton: Hurtig, 1974.

Southerst, John, and Rick Spence. "Gretzky Business." *Profit* Apr.–May 1991: 31–33.

Taylor, Jim. "A Nation in Mourning." *Sports Illustrated* 22 Aug. 1988: 94.

Wallace, Bruce. "Rocket's Red Glare." *Maclean's* 6 May 1991: 38–44.

"Walter Gretzky Still Stable." *Edmonton Journal* 29 Oct. 1991: F3.

Wayne Gretzky: Above and Beyond. Videocassette. Dir. Stuart R. Ross. Ross Sports Productions Inc., 1990.

Wilner, Barry. "The NHL Still Is Wayne's World." *Hockey Digest* June–July 1991: 16–20.

Worldsport Properties. *Canada Cup 1991: The Official History.* Toronto: Worldsport, 1991.

Yuzda, Pamela. "Wayne's World." *Edmonton Journal* 2 Feb. 1992: F1.

Zola, Meguido. *Gretzky! Gretzky! Gretzky!* Toronto: Grolier, 1982.